John Kerry: A Portrait

John Kerry: A Portrait

George Butler

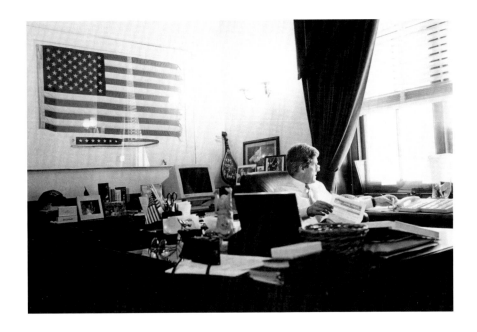

Bulfinch Press

New York   Boston

Bulfinch Press

Time Warner Book Group
1271 Avenue of the Americas
New York, NY 10020
Visit our Web site at www.bulfinchpress.com

First Edition

ISBN 0-8212-6203-3 (hardcover)
ISBN 0-8212-6204-1 (paperback)

Library of Congress Control Number 2004106335

Book and jacket design by Kim Maley

Title page: Senator John Forbes Kerry in his office, Washington, D.C., 1996.

Printed in the United States of America

For Caroline Alexander

"Never for me the lowered banner, never the last endeavour."
– Sir Ernest Shackleton

Also by George Butler

The New Soldier, with Senator John Kerry and David Thorne
Pumping Iron, with Charles Gaines
Pumping Iron II, with Charles Gaines
Arnold Schwarzenegger – A Portrait

John Kerry: A Portrait

Certain memories are as keenly etched as photographs.

MANCHESTER, MASSACHUSETTS. June 1964. An informal lunch before a party. The lunch is being held on a lawn scattered with tables and guests on a spit of land surrounded by the Atlantic Ocean. Waves break in the distance and a sea breeze rustles the leaves of old, well-tended elm trees.

This event was a Bundy family party that included my friend Harvey Bundy and his two uncles, McGeorge and Bill, both high officials in the Kennedy and Johnson administrations. I was standing alone, watching, when a tall figure, rail-thin and Lincolnesque, came across the grass. "Hi, I'm John Kerry," he said simply. We shook hands. I had heard a lot about him from Harvey, who was his roommate, and from two other friends at Yale, David Thorne and Dick Pershing. Specifically, I had heard that John was the youngest president of the Yale Political Union.

During the conversation that followed, I remember thinking: "This man will be President." There was, in John Kerry, a real *presence* that I could feel, and a will that I would grow to appreciate over time.

That summer, long before any political ambitions could be realized, John planned to earn a lot of money in Boston peddling encyclopedias door-to-door. By coincidence, I had my own plan to sell Webster's dictionaries in Dallas, Texas. We had a good laugh over this, neither of us realizing how much more difficult this job would be than the job choice of our college friends: interning in an investment bank.

As we also grew to appreciate, John and I had some things in common. Not the least of these was that we were Brahmins-with-a-catch: although our mothers were from old New England families, our fathers were not. Both had been military men haltered by ill health, side-lined from combat in World War II. Both had lived lives of restless momentum, always traveling. John and I, both active in college, would owe much of our drive, I believe, to the curious fact that both of us began with one foot on each side of an invisible fence.

That night, with lights strung in old elm trees and dark waves breaking at the bottom of the cliffs on which stood the grand house where the party was being held, the dance band played the first fast number of the evening. All the guests started to . . . Charleston. John Kerry, tapping his patent-leather shoes with his fingertips, was easily the best dancer on the floor.

NEW LONDON, CONNECTICUT. June 1966. John invited me to go to the Harvard–Yale crew races. The plan was for Richard Kerry, John's father, to sail his boat *Merlin* to a dock in New London, where we would meet them. In midafternoon, I parked my Volkswagen and saw John, Dick Pershing, and his girlfriend Kitty Hawks already standing on the dock loading some baskets of food onto *Merlin*.

In fine, hazy evening light, we sailed out onto the estuary of the Connecticut River to watch the contest. Harvard was favored in all boats. This did not seem to deter John or Dick. "A better view is needed," said Dick. "To the top of the mainmast," replied John. The two friends skillfully climbed the old wooden mast, where they balanced precariously on the spar. However, the cheerleading efforts of Kerry and Pershing could not improve the Yale crews as they lost race after race.

When the races were over, the group assembled a picnic and ate hamburgers cooked over a charcoal grill. Kerry and Pershing amused themselves by reciting alternate verses of Kipling's "Gunga Din" in excellent Cockney accents.

"Din! Din! Din!" was Pershing's refrain.

I knew he was going into the 101st Airborne Division. What I did not know was that this would be the last time I would see him.

CHICAGO, ILLINOIS. August 1966. The day blazed with sunshine. It was hot and still on the deck of a yacht club on the shore of Lake Michigan. This was a lunch in honor of Harvey Bundy and his bride-to-be, Blakely Fetridge. John Kerry was sitting at the head of a table, looking pensive. He would not be able to attend the wedding, because today, in the early afternoon, he was taking a plane back to Boston. Early the following morning he would be inducted into the Navy.

There was much discussion of the Vietnam war at the table. Once again, the party included prominent administration elders who were vocal in their encouragement for us to volunteer for duty. Additionally, I — who was going on to graduate school — was subtly approached by a CIA official about future service.

Then lunch was coming to an end. John looked up at the skyline of Chicago. "Yesterday," John said, "George and I rented a plane and I flew him right along this shore. What an amazing city . . ."

It was time for him to go. There was much handshaking and good-luck wishing.

From the deck, I watched him enter a taxi to report for duty at the Naval War College.

We have always stayed in touch since our first encounter in the summer of 1964. John wrote me from Vietnam. I replied first from New York, where I was working for *Newsweek,* then from Detroit, where I was in my own version of a war in "Murder City." It was while I was living in the ghetto that I took up photography and eventually, when I came to Boston to work for John, took his campaign's publicity photos. I did so because there was no one else to do it.

These photos began as utility pictures. Then, as I developed as a photographer, they became a record (and, along the way, a book, when Kerry, Thorne, and I published a volume called *The New Soldier* in 1971).

As an ongoing record, they illustrate many things about John Kerry. But now, looking at a whole book of photos that have never been printed until these last few months (who would publish photos of John Kerry before he won the primaries in Iowa and New Hampshire in January 2004?), what stands out are the humble beginnings of a career, the sense that this was going to be a long slog, the wholly unglamorous daily life of a young political candidate. Only willpower, pure willpower, kept Kerry going on more occasions than I care to remember. His career would be marked by diligence, absolute determination, raw idealism, and absolute disregard for bad polling numbers or any obstruction.

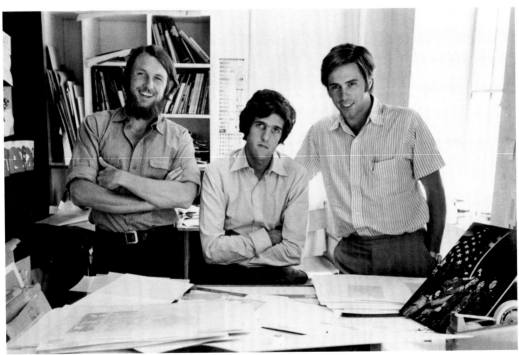

Michael Abramson

George Butler, John Kerry, and David Thorne.

The author photo for our book, *The New Soldier*, a chronicle of Vietnam Veterans Against the War during Operation Dewey Canyon III, July 1971.

It is always a long slog. In late 2003, when John was at his nadir and I had an assignment to photograph him, I could barely look through my Leica, so ravaged and tired was the face I saw in my viewfinder. But even then, as I kept telling often impatient and incredulous parties, "John is a great closer. Watch him in the stretch."

I'd seen the arc of Kerry's life. I knew he was tough as steel.

This is my photographic record of my experience with John Kerry. It began long ago at a party that might be described as the end of an era. It's ended in a hard-earned presidential race in an entirely new world.

Holderness, New Hampshire
May 2004

Early Political Life

John Kerry was born on December 11, 1943. He was twenty-six years old, a heavily decorated Vietnam war hero, and just out of the Navy when he made his entry into politics.

John Kerry wanted to run for Congress so he could lead the fight to end the Vietnam War, drawing on his special credibility as some-one who had served there honorably. He declared his candidacy in the Third Congressional District in Massachusetts, where antiwar constituents were holding a caucus to select a strong candidate to run against incumbent Democrat Philip Philbin, a conservative hawk.

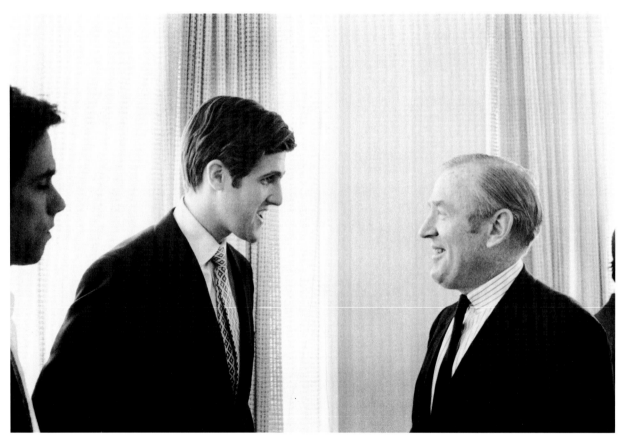

David Thorne, John Kerry, and Paul B. Fay, Jr. Logan Airport, Boston, January 1970.

Paul Fay was Under Secretary of the Navy under President Kennedy. The idea behind this picture, one of my earliest of John Kerry, was to get some attention for John. This was attention by association.

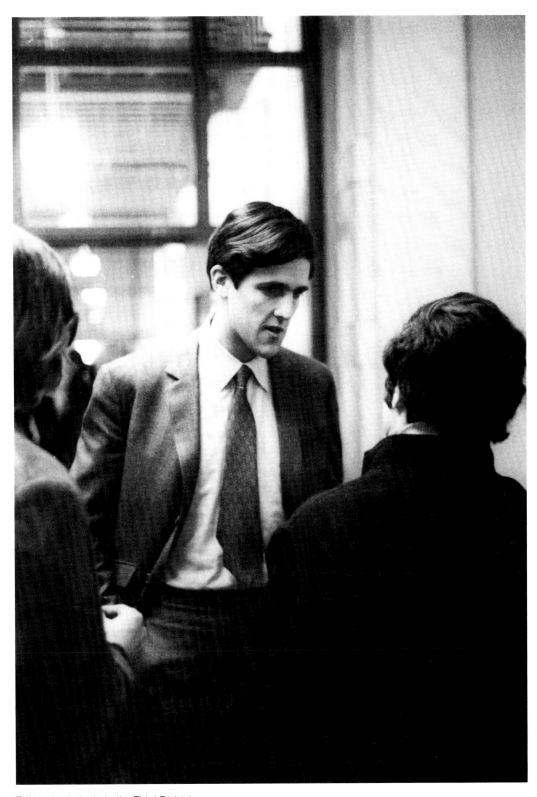

Talking to students in the Third District.

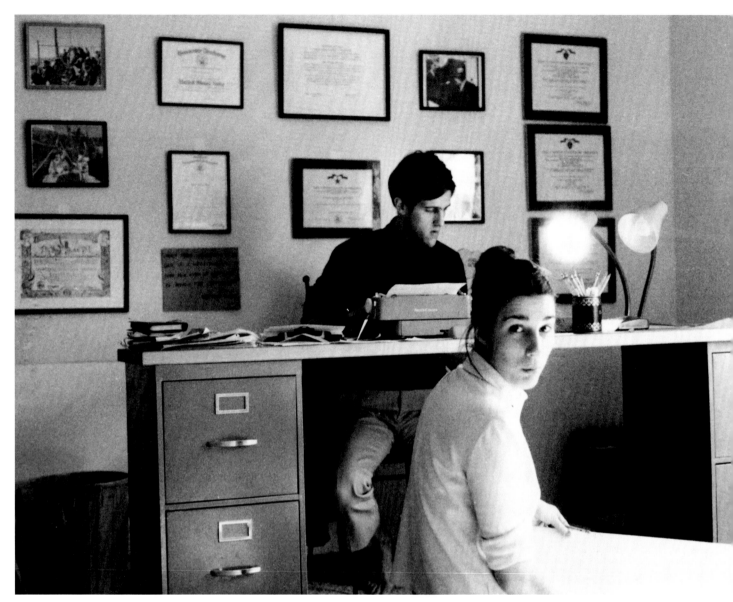

John Kerry and Julia Thorne.

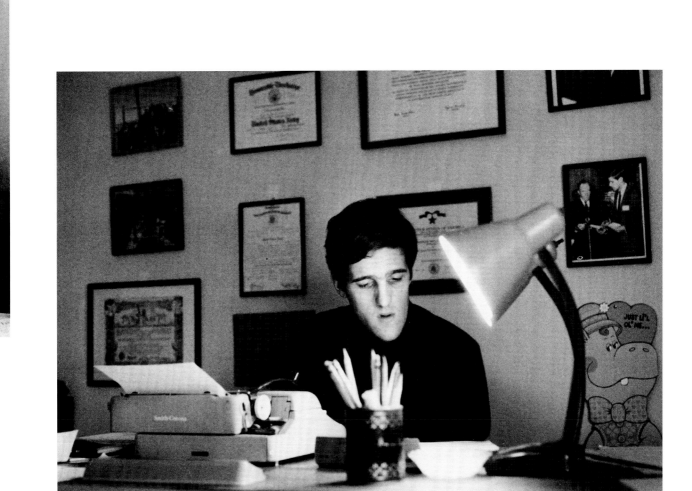

John Kerry's earliest political organizing was done out of the cellar of a rented house in Waltham, Massachusetts. He wrote his own letters and speeches. Julia Thorne, his fiancée (and David Thorne's twin sister), was involved from the outset.

The Third District Caucus

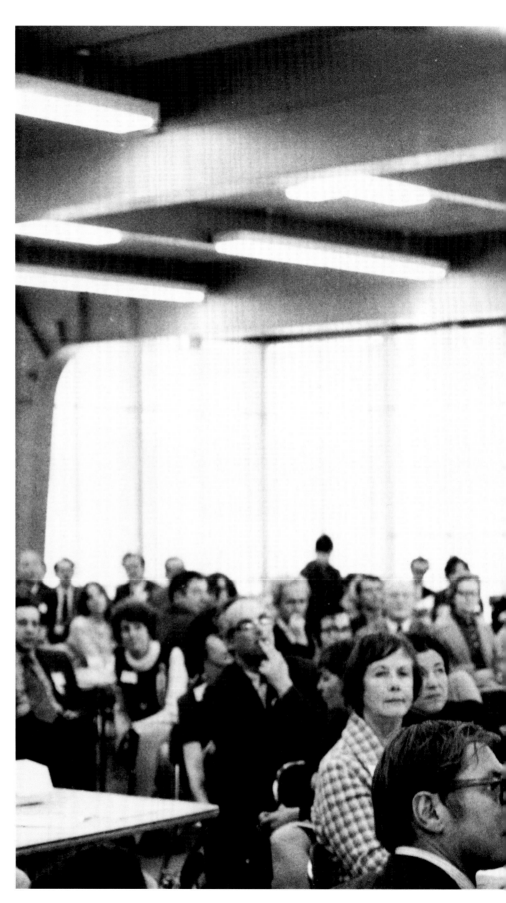

In the auditorium of Concord-Carlisle High School, some seventeen miles outside of Boston, two thousand members of a "Citizens' Caucus" were determined to use old-fashioned politics to help end the war in Vietnam by sending a peace candidate to Congress.

John Kerry, February 22, 1970.

14

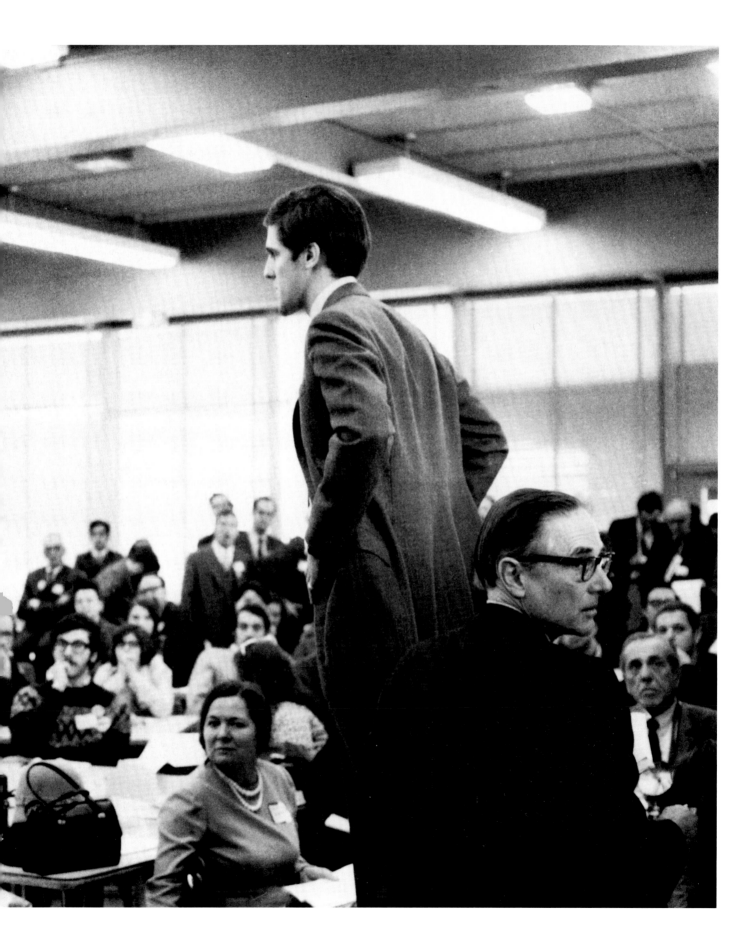

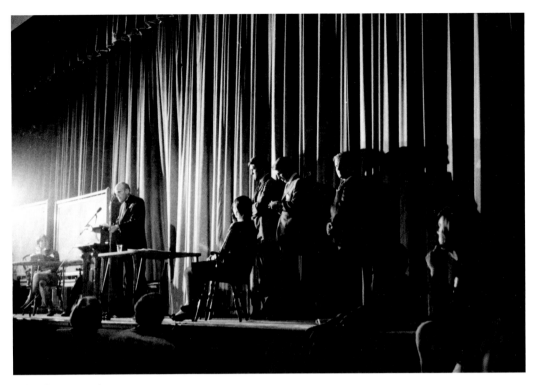

Father Drinan speaks.

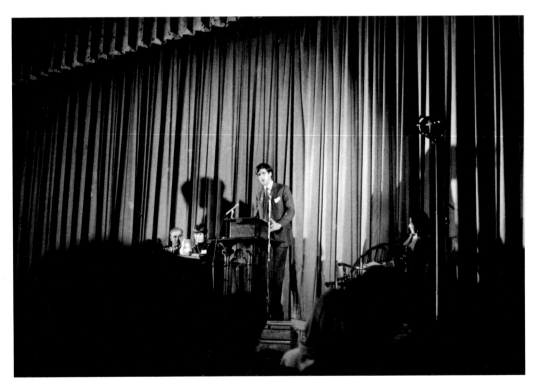

John Kerry speaks.

John's opponent in the caucus was Father Robert F. Drinan, a Jesuit priest and dean of Boston College Law School. Drinan was a distinguished man and by far the favorite of the organizers of the antiwar caucus. Therefore, the "Kerry Kids," as we were known (all in our early twenties), had to work harder to get John Kerry a victory in the caucus.

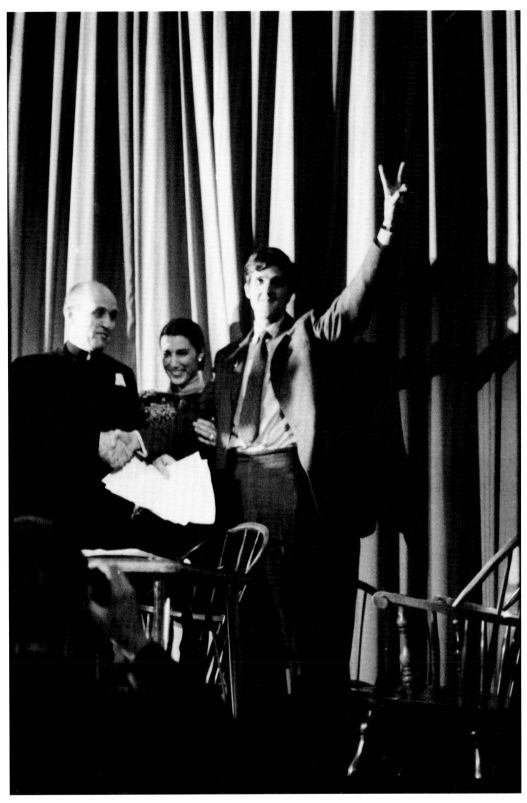

A victory for Drinan nevertheless brought Kerry to the attention of the peace movement — and Massachusetts voters.

Wedding of John Kerry and Julia Stimson Thorne

Bay Shore, New York, May 23, 1970

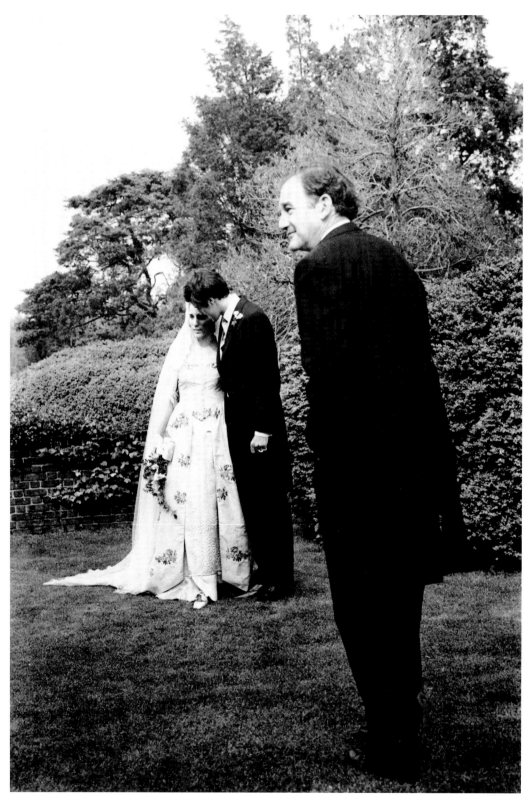

A wedding portrait with Richard Kerry, father of the groom.

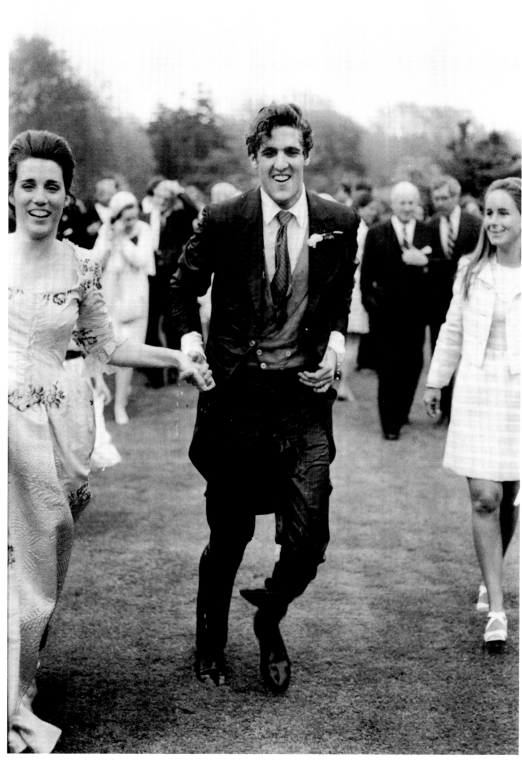

John Kerry, dripping wet after being thrown in the pond by his groomsmen.

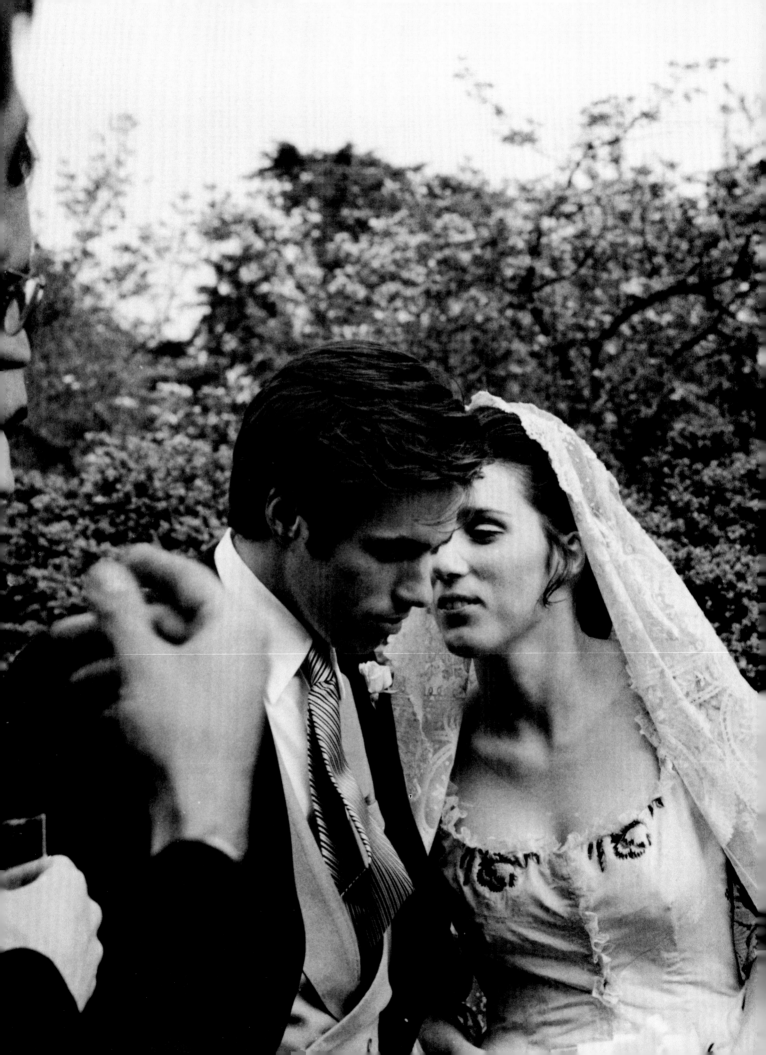

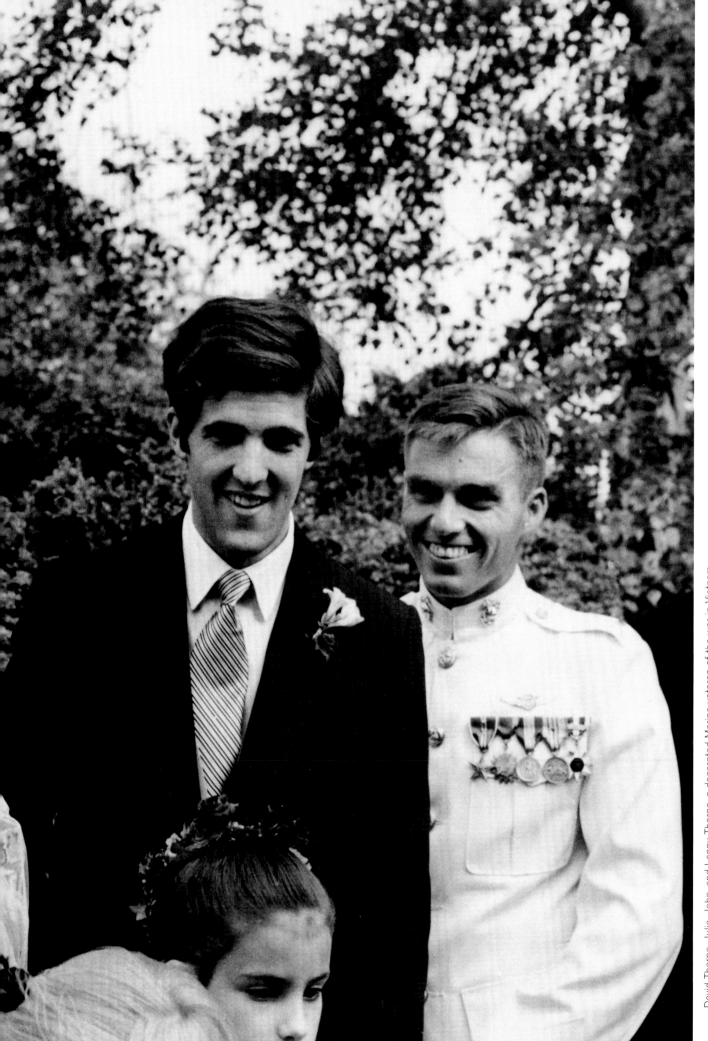

David Thorne, Julia, John, and Lanny Thorne, a decorated Marine veteran of the war in Vietnam.

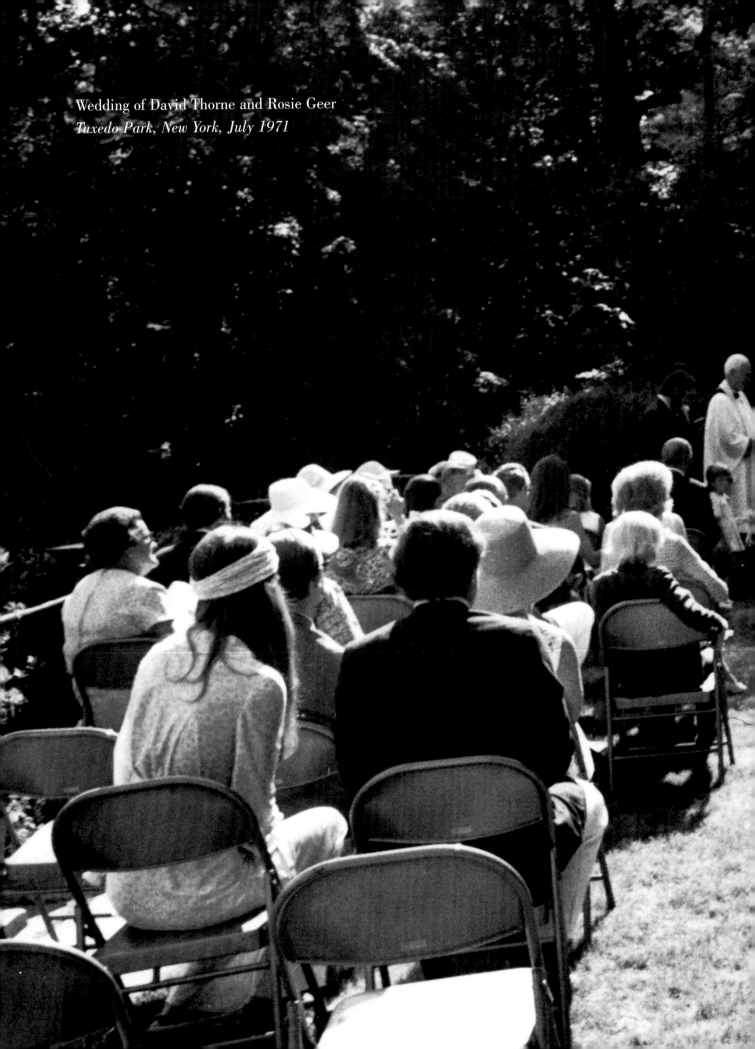

Wedding of David Thorne and Rosie Geer
Tuxedo Park, New York, July 1971

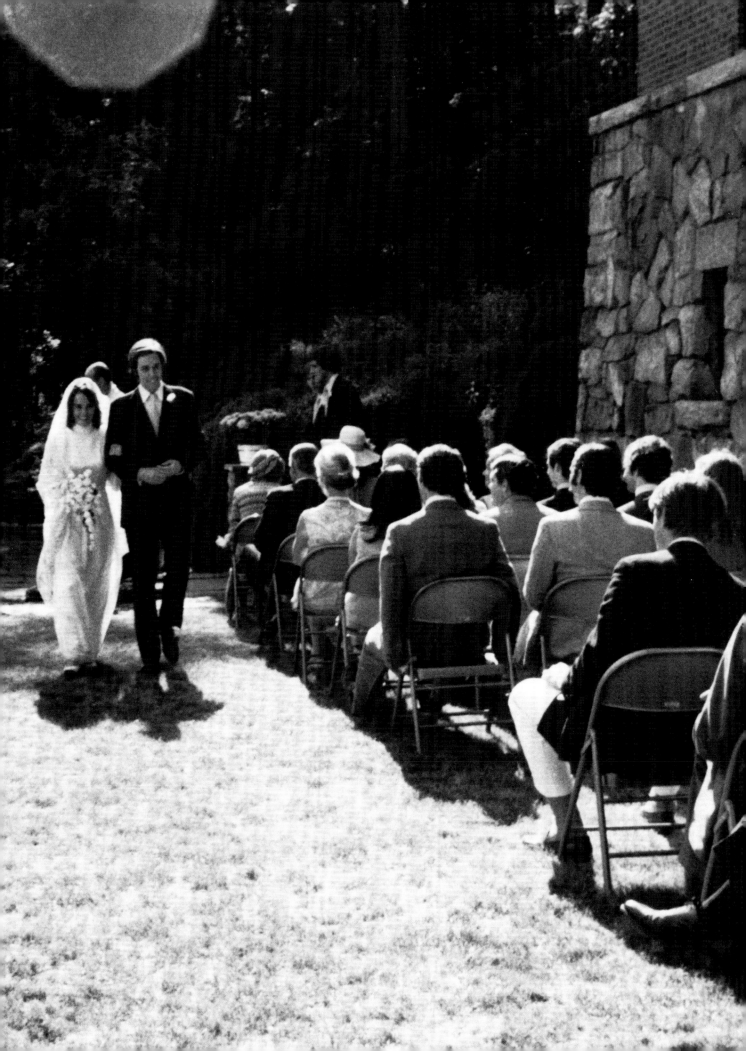

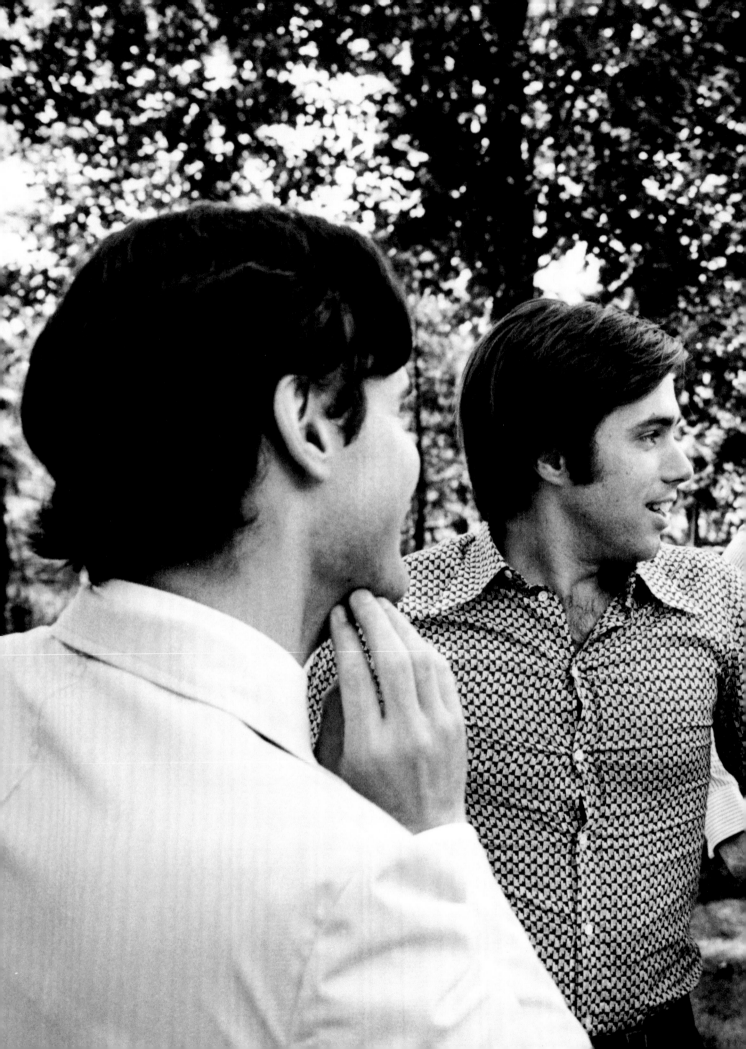

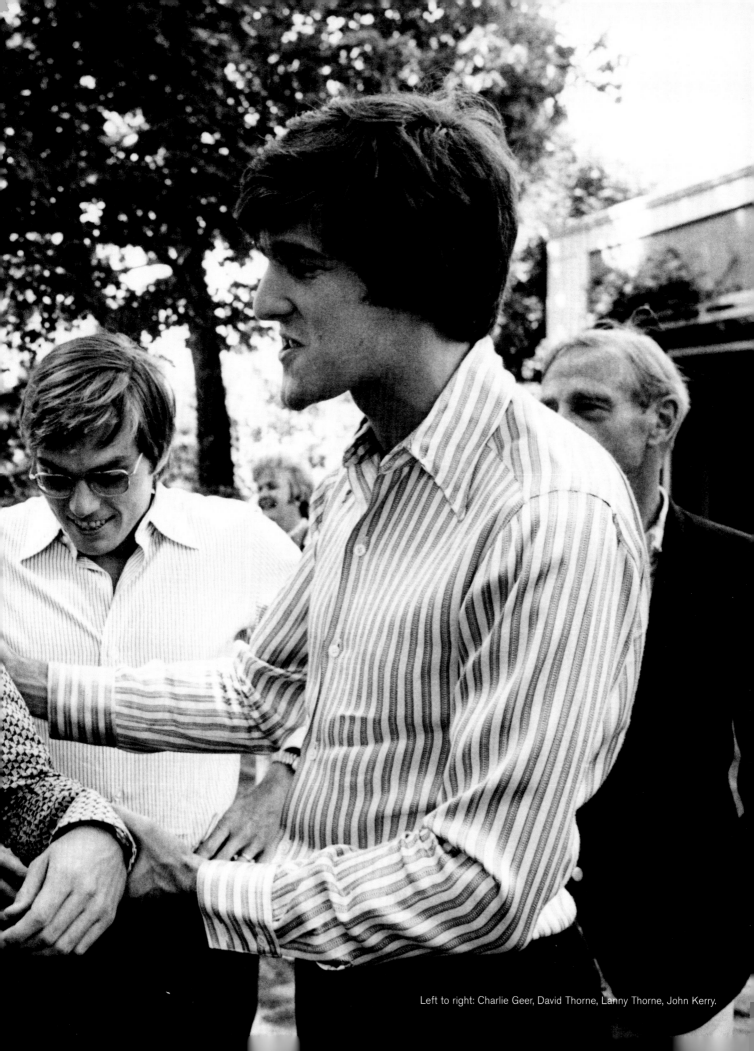

Left to right: Charlie Geer, David Thorne, Lanny Thorne, John Kerry.

Vietnam Veterans' Gathering

Detroit, Michigan, January 31–February 2, 1971

About a hundred and fifty Vietnam veterans gather at a Howard Johnson Motor Lodge to talk about the painful experiences and unshakable memories of their tours in Vietnam. This testimony was highly charged and revealing. But perhaps because the event was underfinanced and underpublicized, it did not receive much national press coverage.

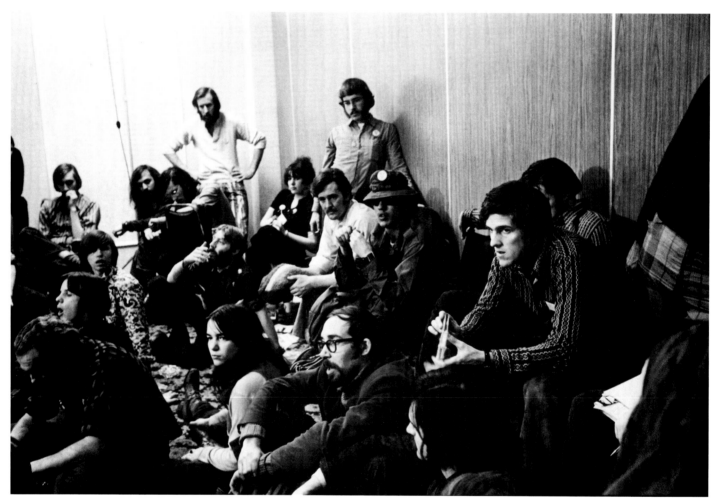

John Kerry was uncertain whether he wanted to get involved. He invited me to come with him to check it out, as I had been a VISTA volunteer in Detroit and was living in the North End, adjacent to where the event was held, working on a lengthy photo project. Sitting in front of John is Jan Crumb, who was a national leader of Vietnam Veterans Against the War.

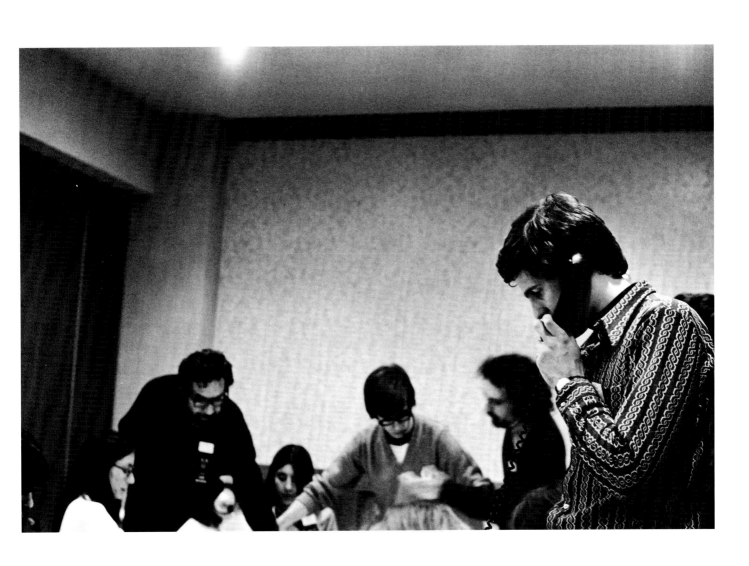

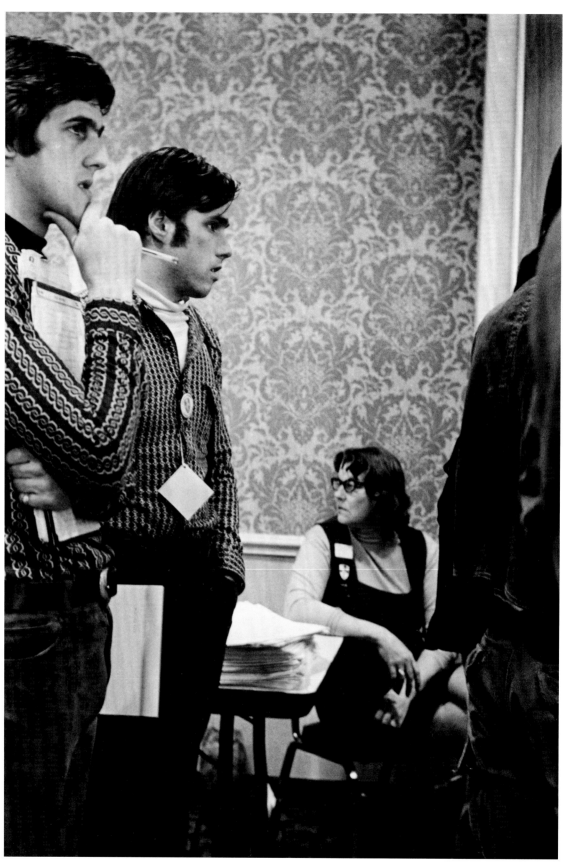

John, David, and I were taken aback by the testimony of real veterans — who had gone to Vietnam for patriotic reasons — testifying about their activities in a war gone wrong.

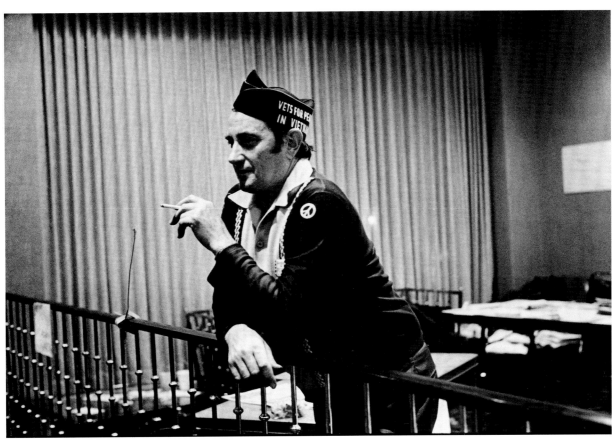

On the last day of the investigation, a plan was discussed for a Vietnam Veterans Against the War March on Washington that would draw national attention. This march was called "Dewey Canyon III," an ironic reference to the two U.S.-backed invasions of Laos.

Dewey Canyon III:

"A limited incursion into the country of Congress"

Dewey Canyon I was an invasion of Laos by the 3rd Marine Division in January 1969.
Dewey Canyon II was an invasion of Laos in February 1971 by South Vietnamese forces.

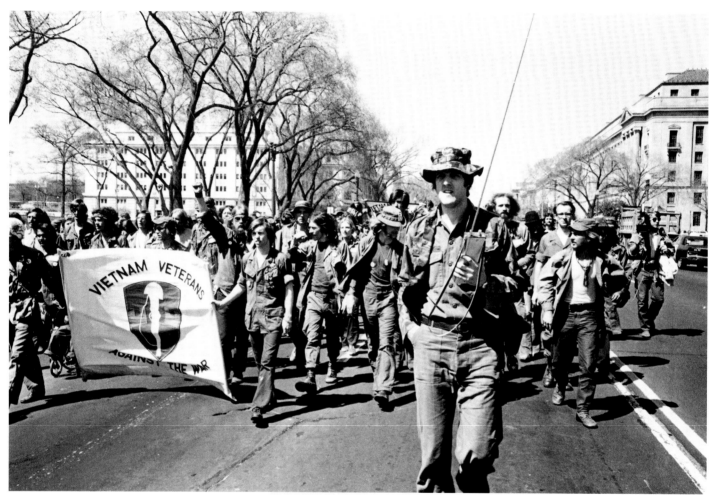

Monday, April 19, 1971, about eleven hundred vets march, some in wheelchairs, some on crutches, from Arlington National Cemetery to the Capitol. John raised a lot of money for the vets by speaking to various groups. He also gave a strong presentation on *Meet the Press* concerning the motives for the March on Washington. But most of all, his strength of character and his history as a highly decorated combat veteran made him one of the top leaders of the Vietnam Veterans Against the War on their first day in Washington.

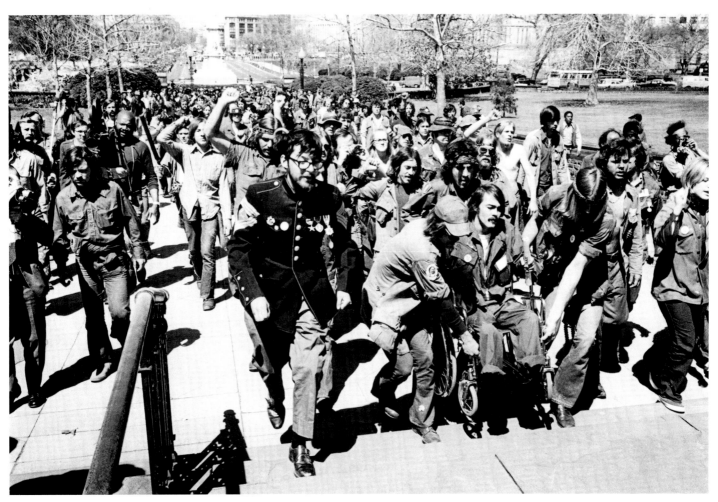

After being locked out of Arlington National Cemetery by the Nixon administration, veterans who had served their country marched peacefully to the steps of Congress.

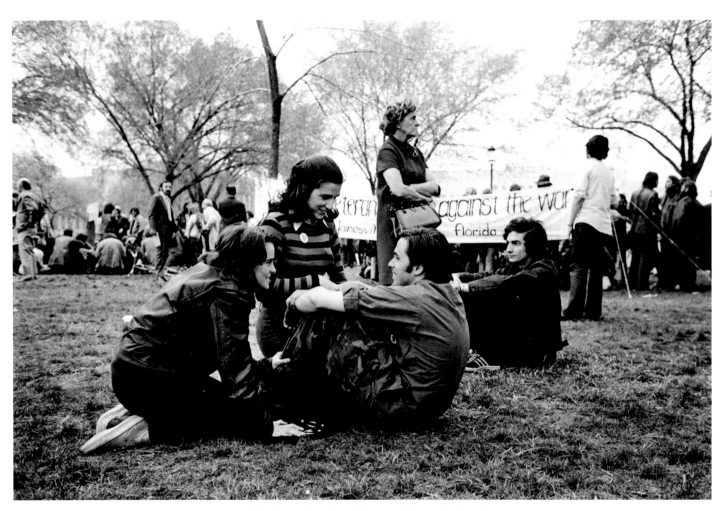

Left to right: Rose Thorne, Julia Kerry, David Thorne, Cam Kerry. Standing is Rosemary Kerry, John's mother.

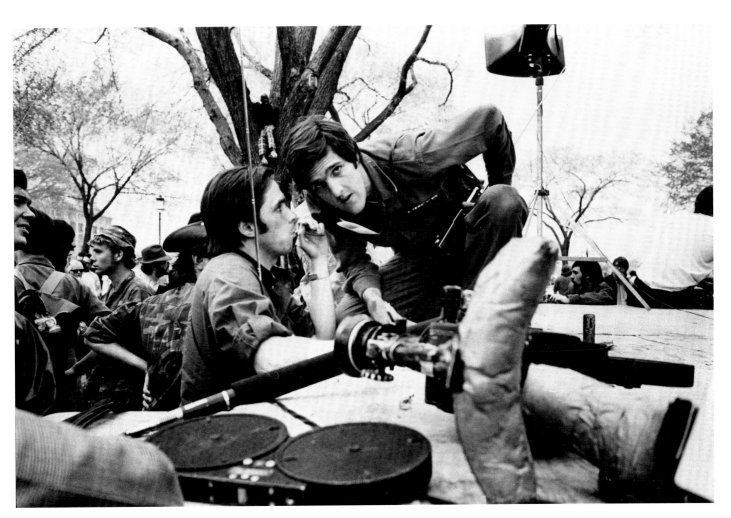

David Thorne confers with John Kerry.

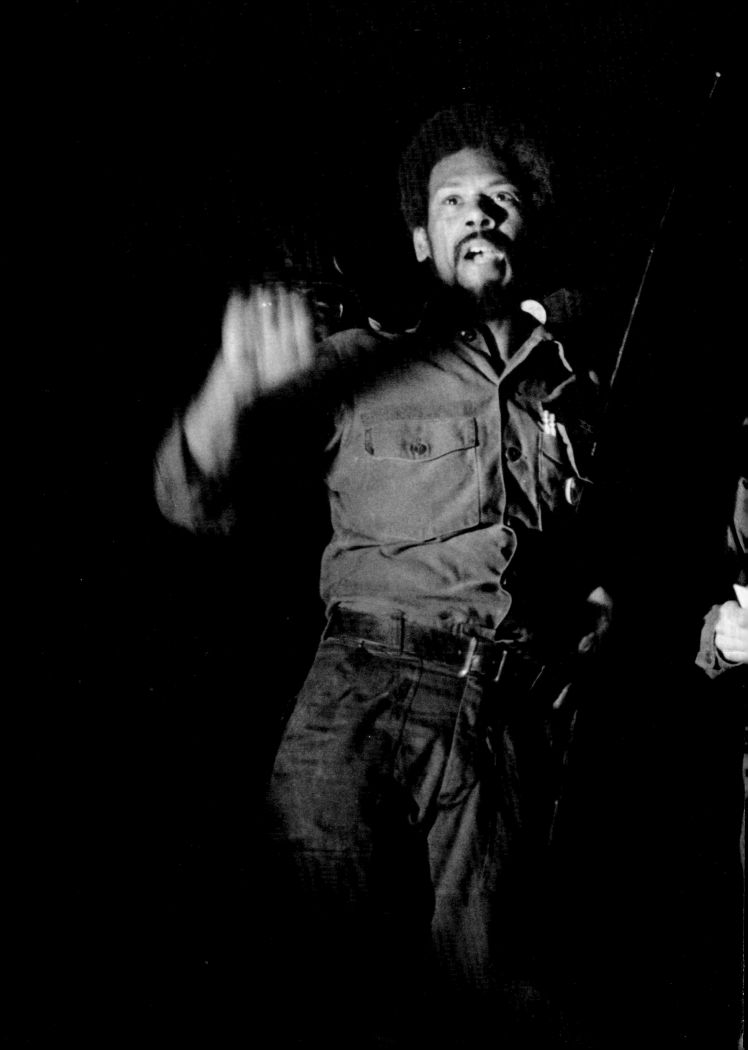

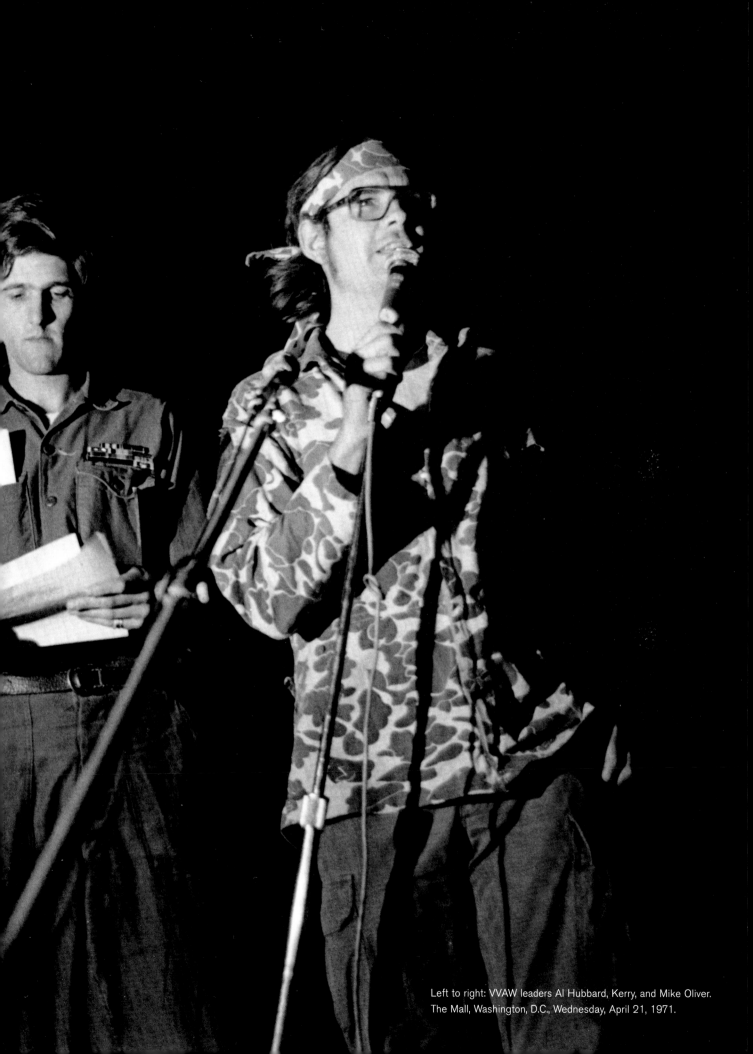

Left to right: VVAW leaders Al Hubbard, Kerry, and Mike Oliver.
The Mall, Washington, D.C., Wednesday, April 21, 1971.

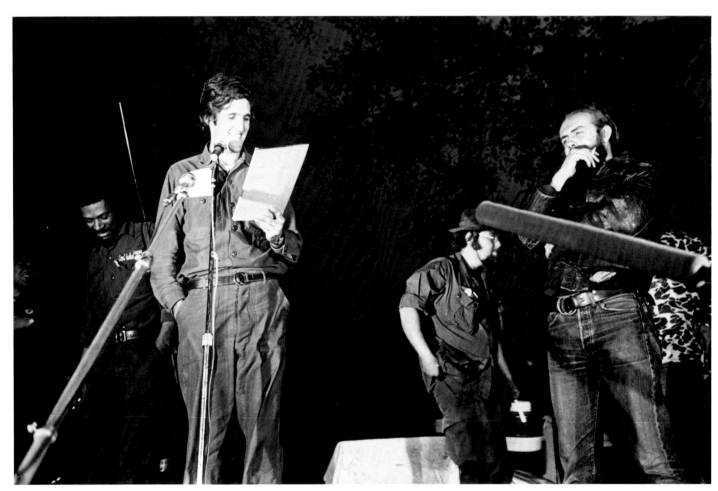

The Supreme Court offered the veterans a curious option: Stay on the Mall but don't sleep. Sleep on the Mall and be arrested. The veterans voted 480 to 400 to sleep on the Mall. Here John announces the decision. Washington police, siding with the veterans, declined to arrest any of the sleeping vets.

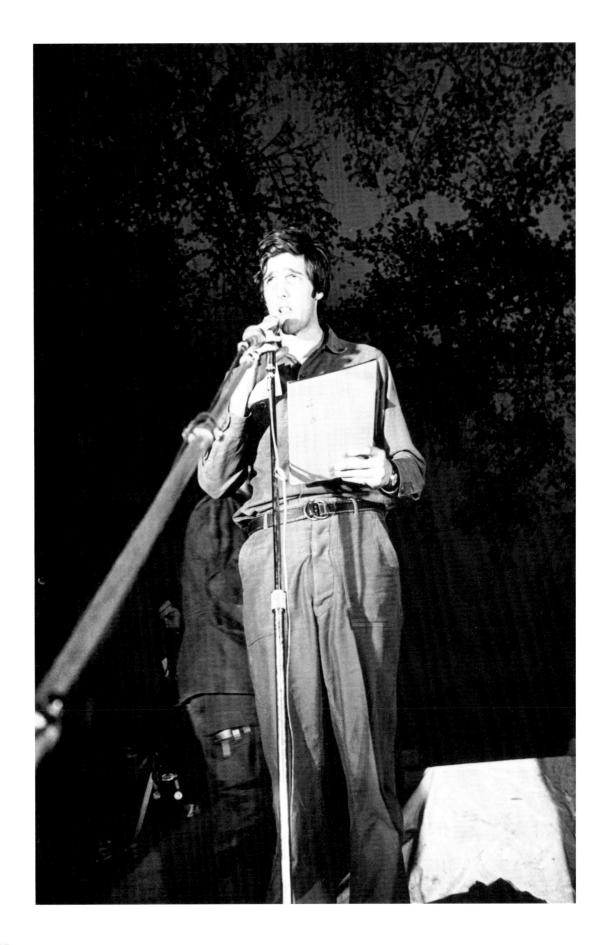

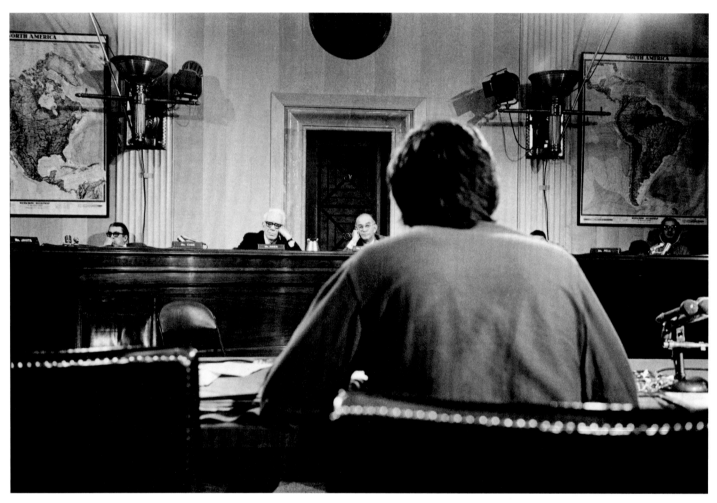

John Kerry testifies before the Senate Foreign Relations Committee. This speech was broadcast on the news around the world, bringing Kerry instant renown.

"How do you ask a man to be the last man to die in Vietnam? How do you ask a man to be the last man to die for a mistake?" asked John Kerry as part of his eloquent testimony, April 22, 1971.

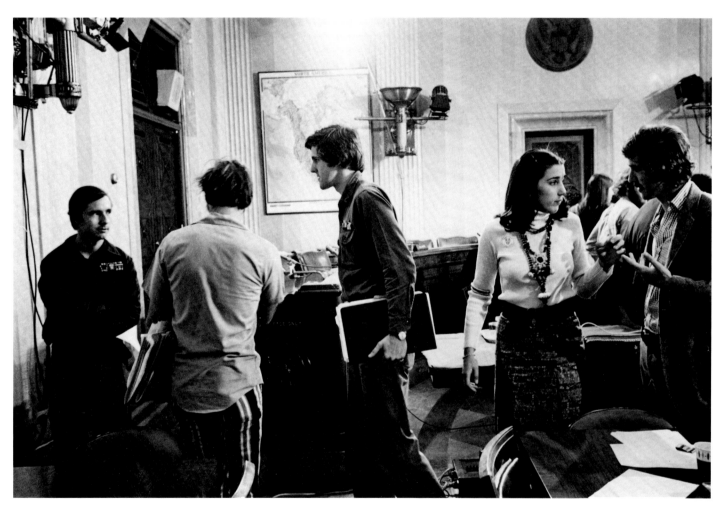

After his testimony, John, who had been up all night writing his speech, finally gets a moment of relief.

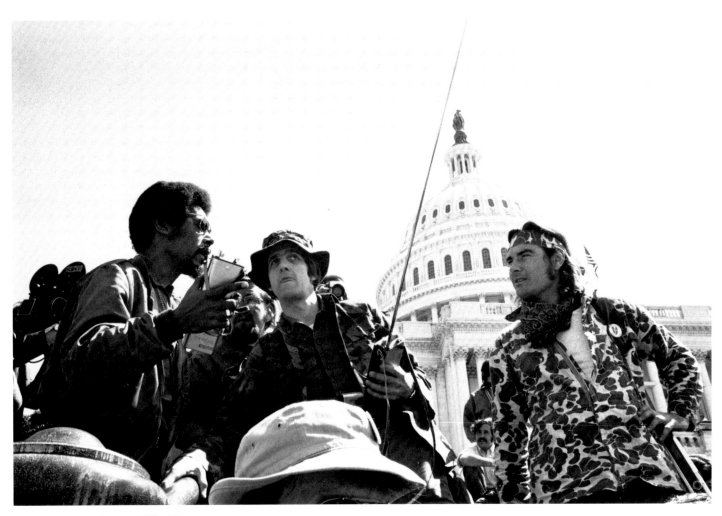

Al Hubbard, John Kerry, and Mike Oliver.

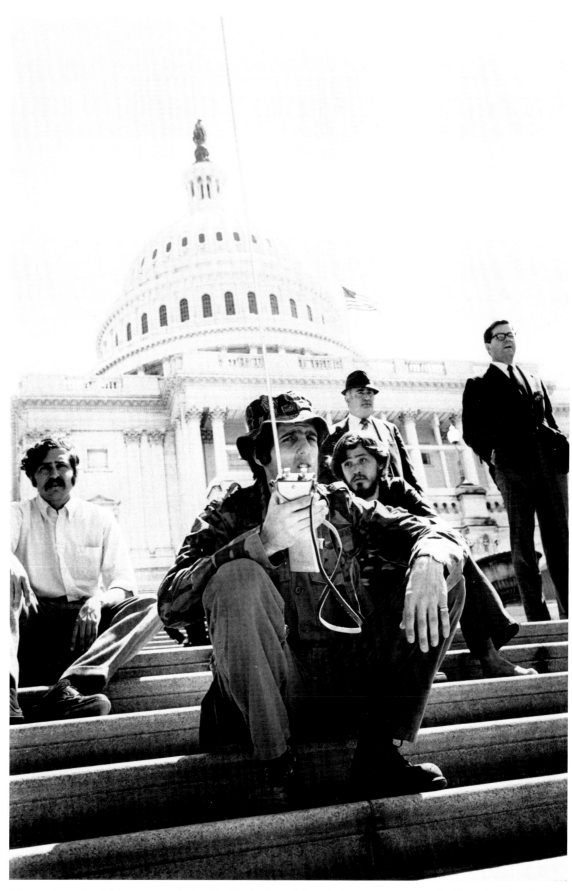

John used a walkie-talkie to communicate with other leaders of the vets. There was a concern that impostors placed by the government might try to provoke violence.

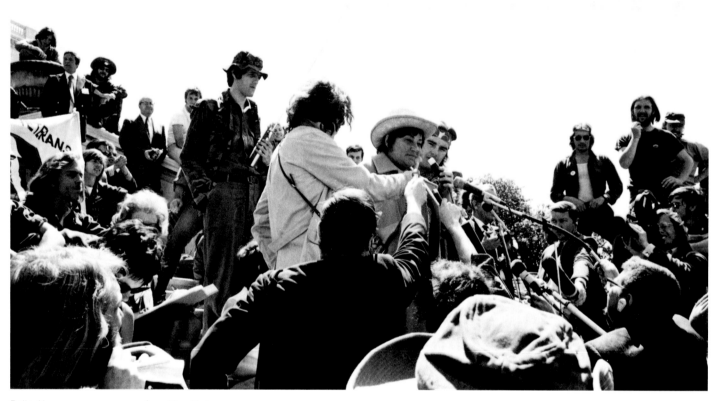

Bella Abzug, congresswoman from New York.

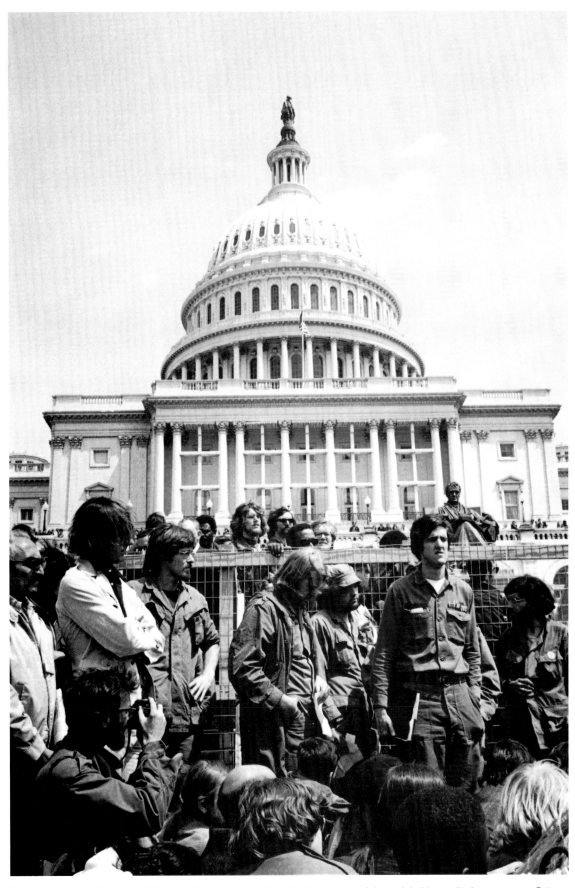

The veterans staged a powerfully symbolic ceremony — throwing their war medals, medal ribbons, discharge papers, Saigon driver's licenses, and other Vietnam war tokens onto the Capitol steps. Before doing so, each veteran spoke to the gathered crowd. Here, John Kerry waits in line.

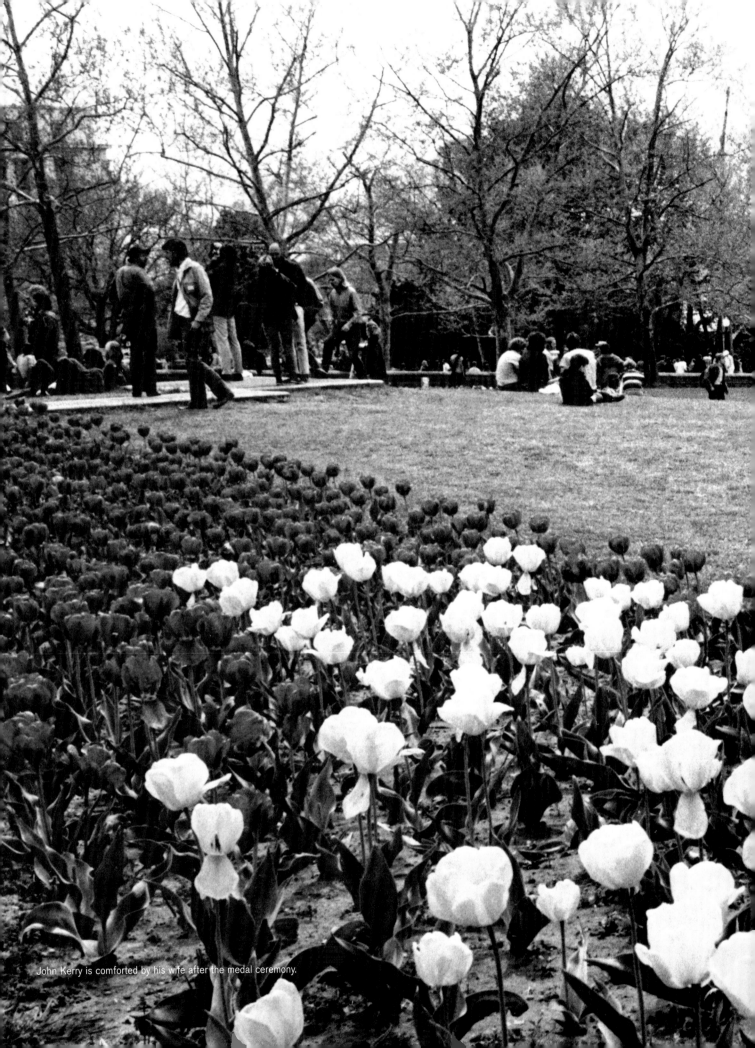

John Kerry is comforted by his wife after the medal ceremony.

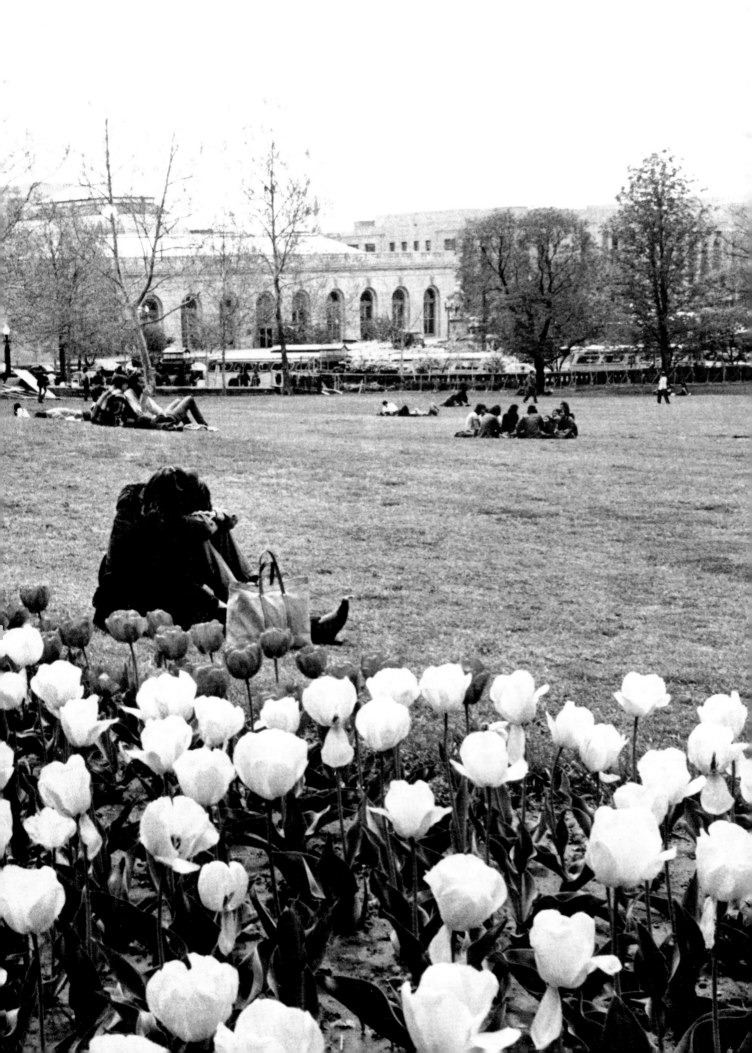

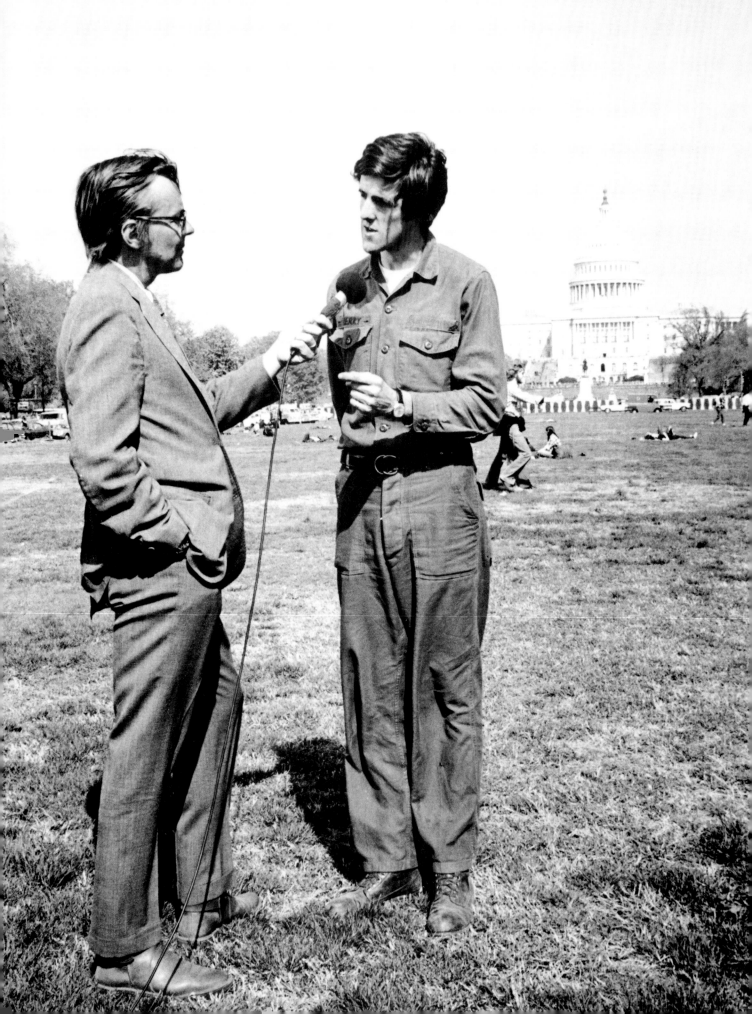

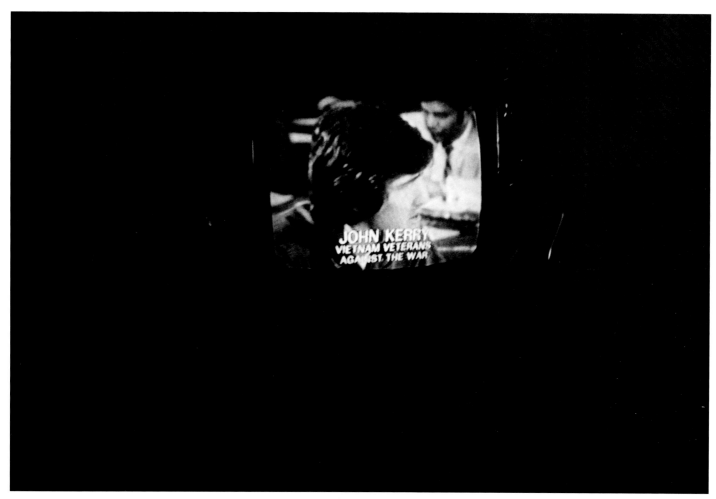

John Kerry on the evening news, April 22, 1971.

Correspondent Bruce Morton interviews John Kerry.

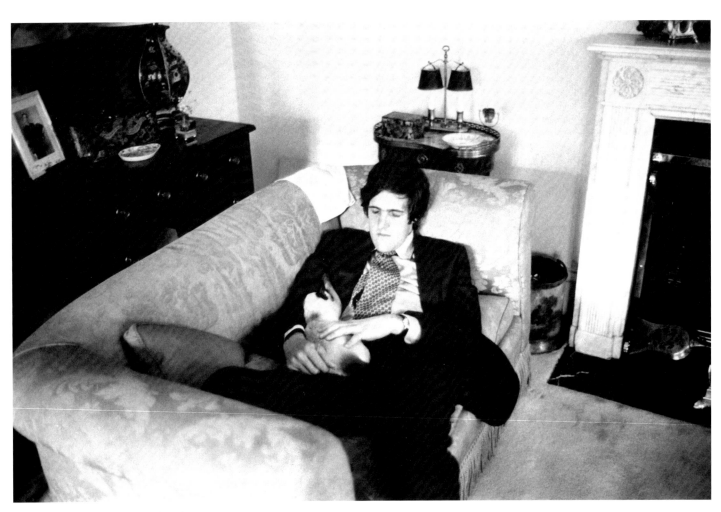

John with his cat, Sunday, April 25, 1971.

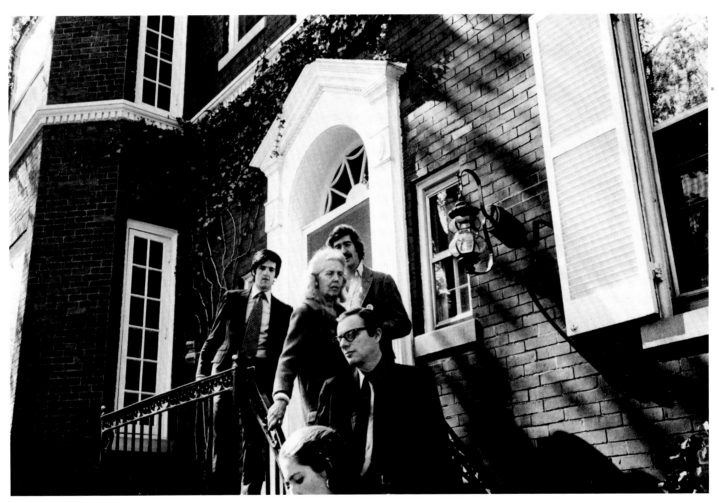

John Kerry leaves Kay Halle's house after a lunch with Washington officials.

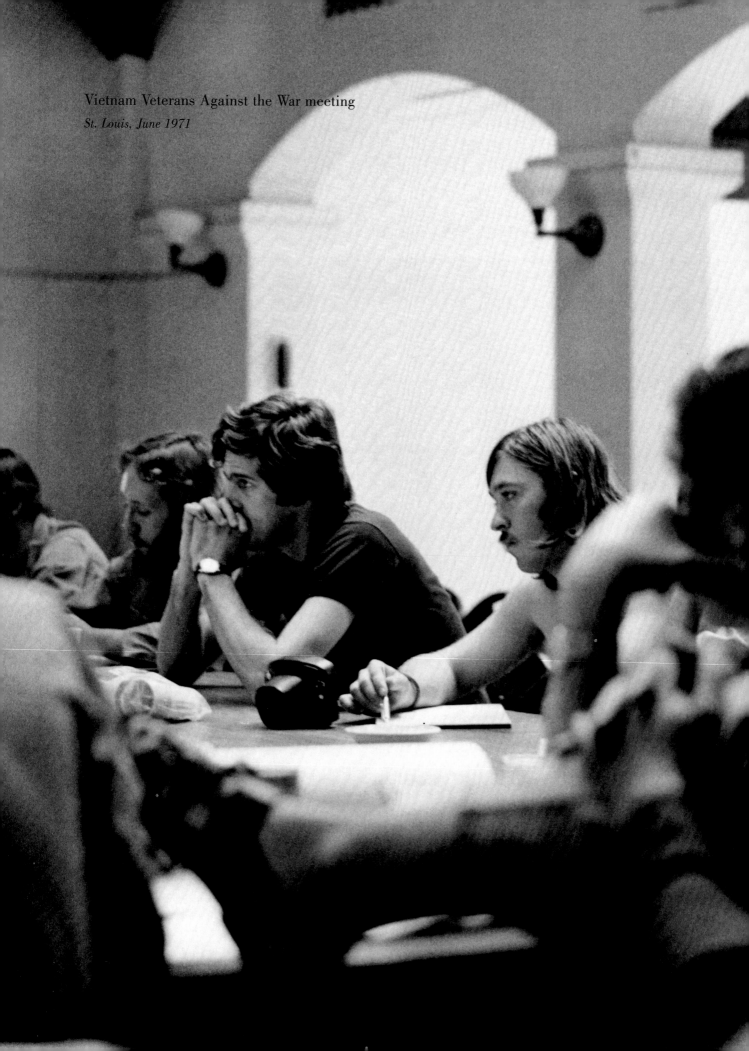

Vietnam Veterans Against the War meeting
St. Louis, June 1971

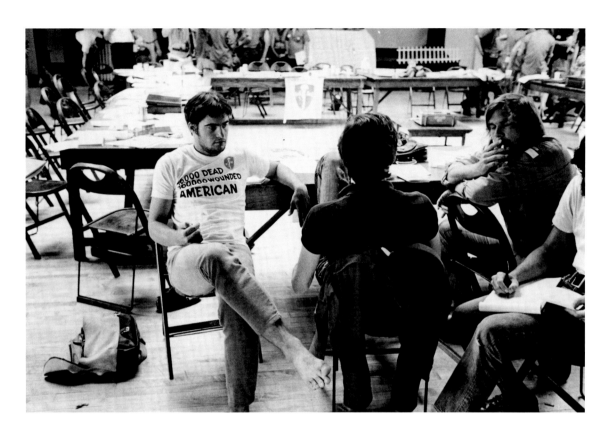

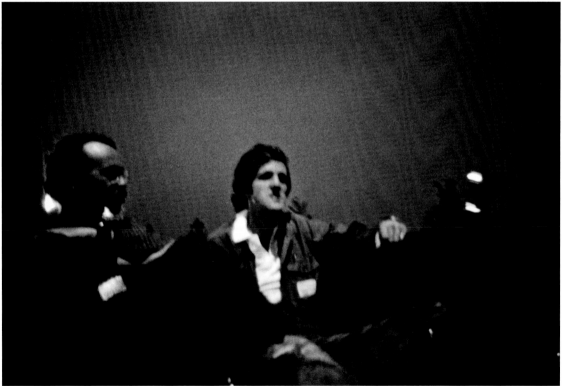

John riding in the back of a pickup truck, St. Louis, Missouri, June 1971.

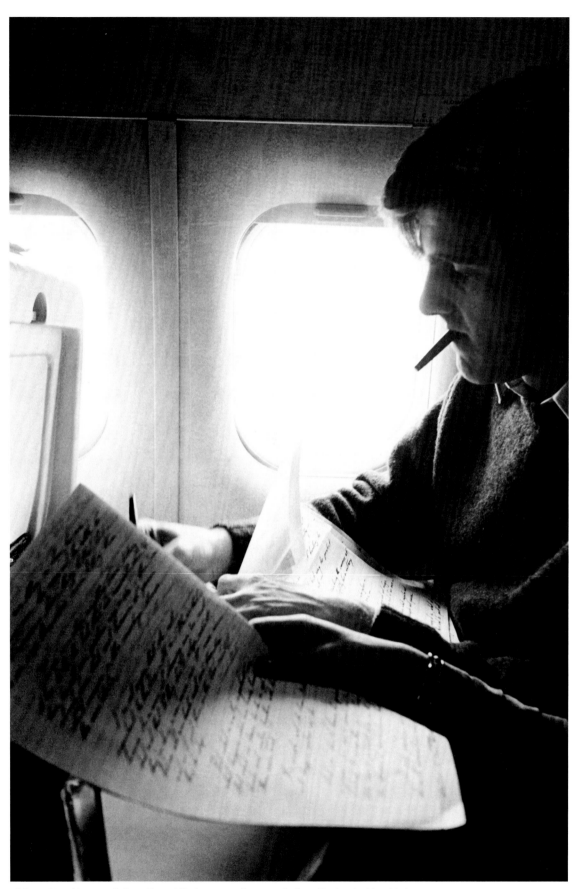

John writing his speech for a Bryant Park peace rally en route from Boston to New York.

Peace Rally, Bryant Park

New York City, April 22, 1972

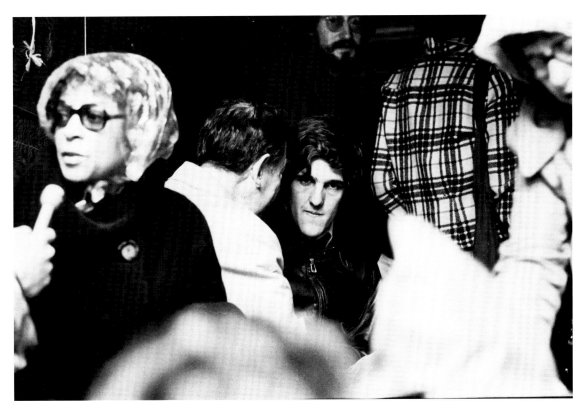

Kerry huddles with an organizer

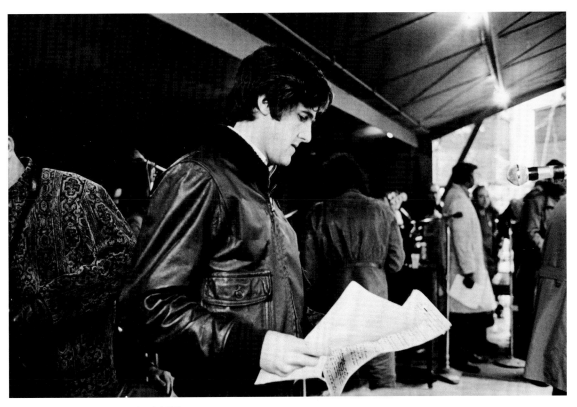

… and reviews his speech, April 1972.

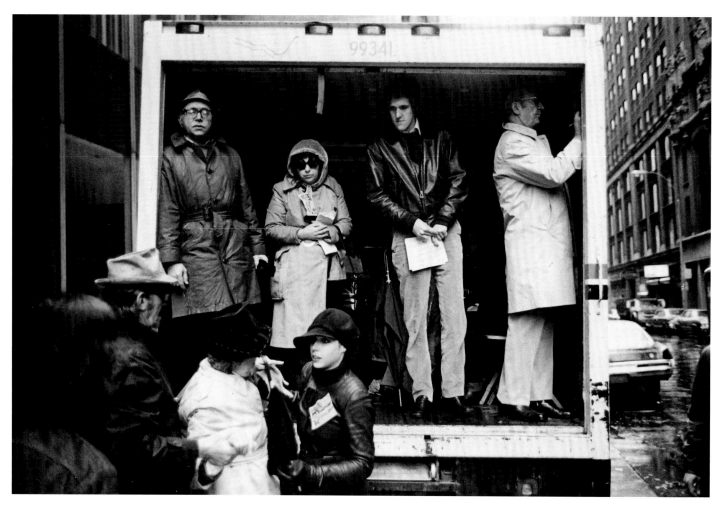

Shelter from the rain. Kerry waits to speak.

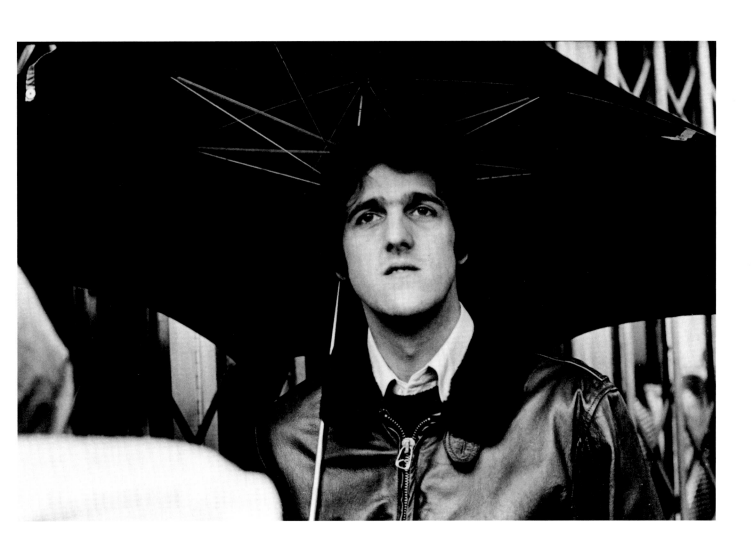

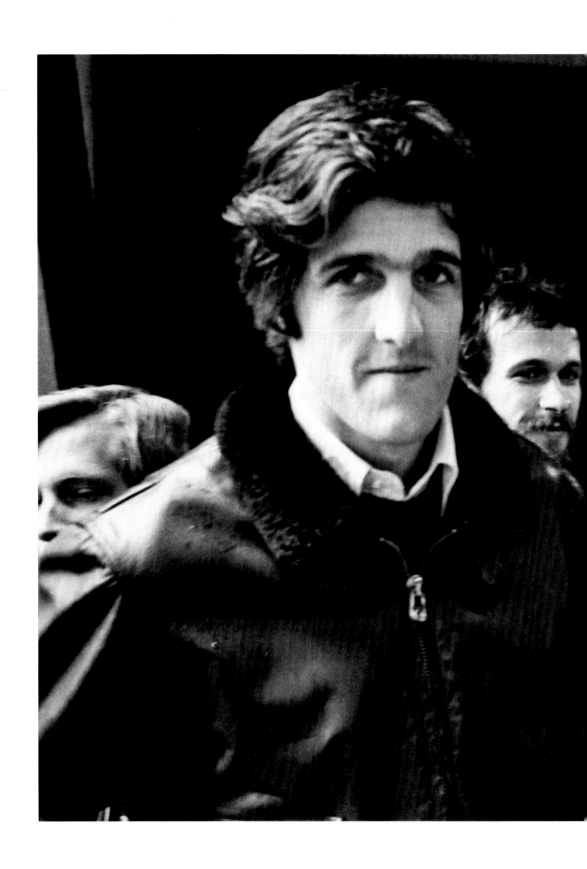

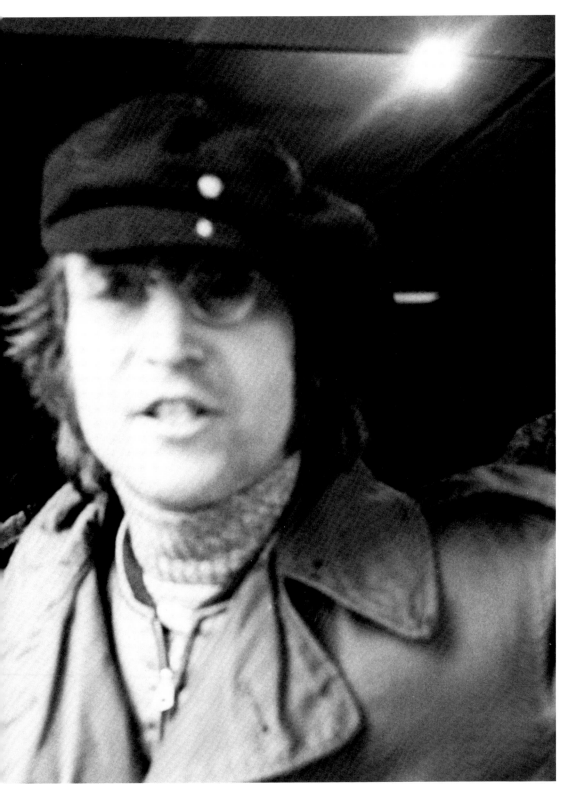

John Kerry and John Lennon.

The back of a rented truck kept John and me sheltered from the rain as we waited for the rally to begin. I heard the hydraulic lift on the truck rising behind me and turned. Standing on the the lift were Lennon and Yoko Ono, levitating mystically in front of me. The lift reached its full height, and as Lennon stepped by me, I called out his name. He turned and I took this picture.

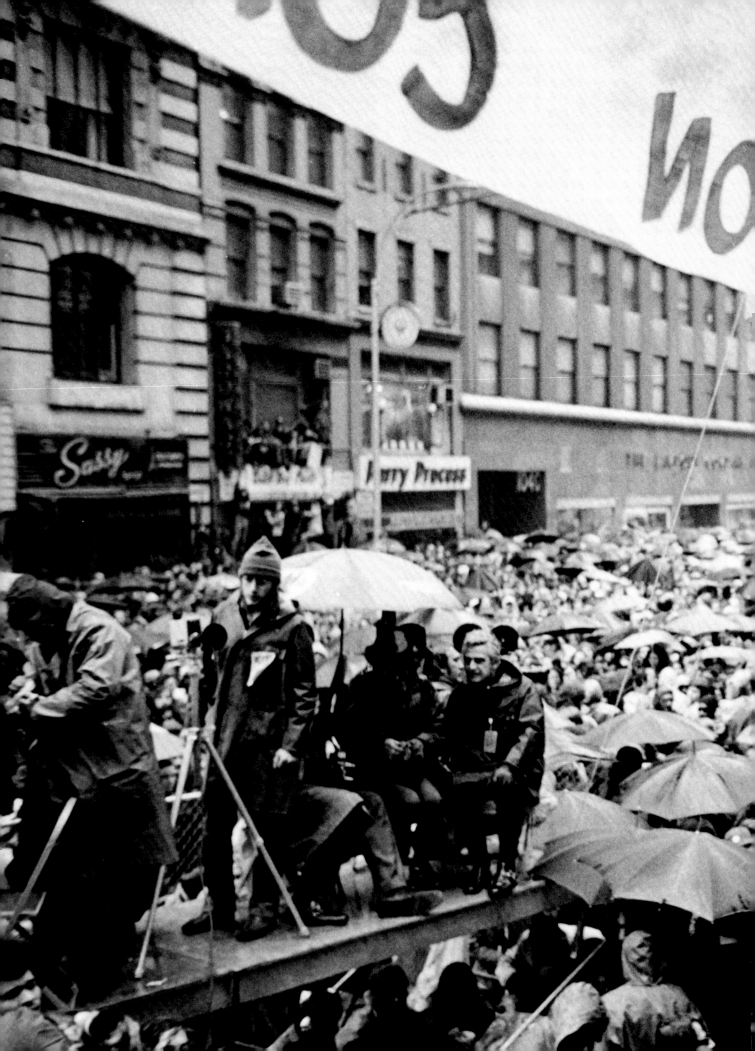

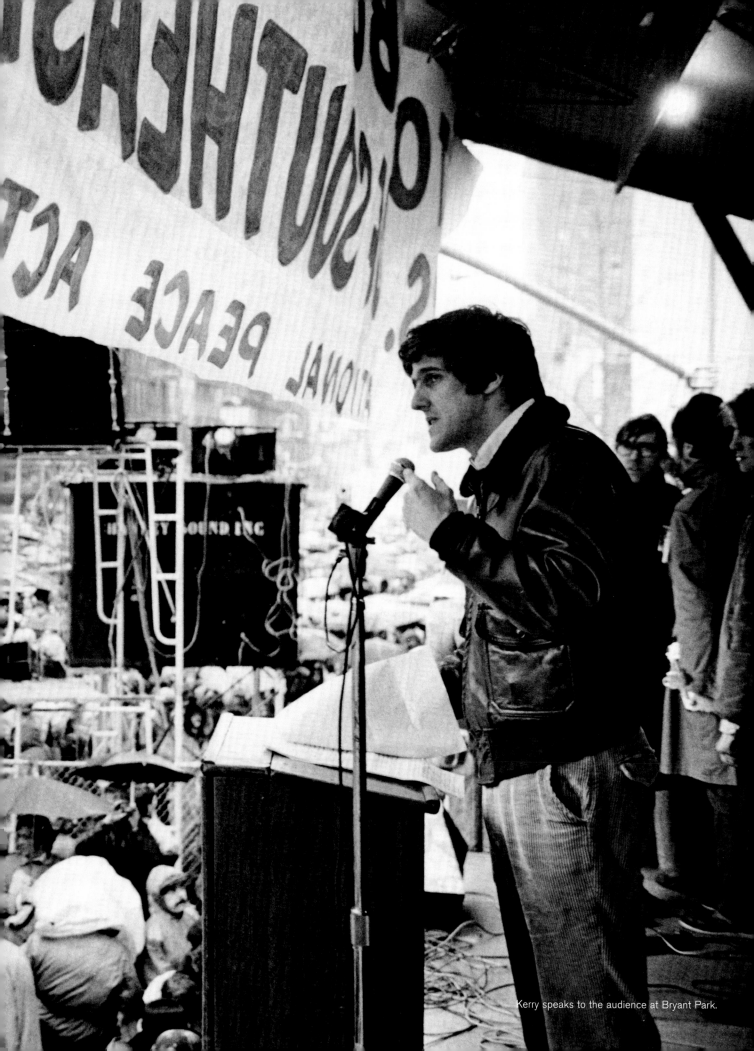

Kerry speaks to the audience at Bryant Park.

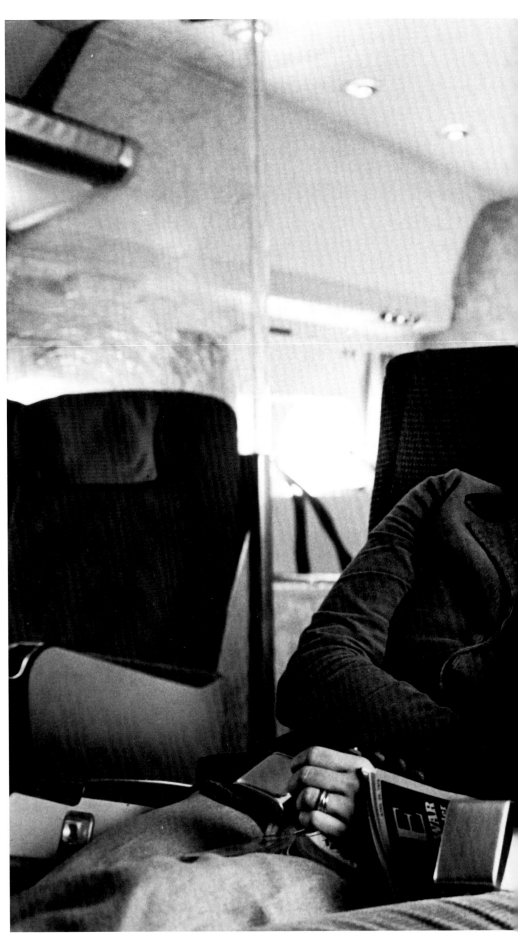

Julia and John Kerry return home from New York.

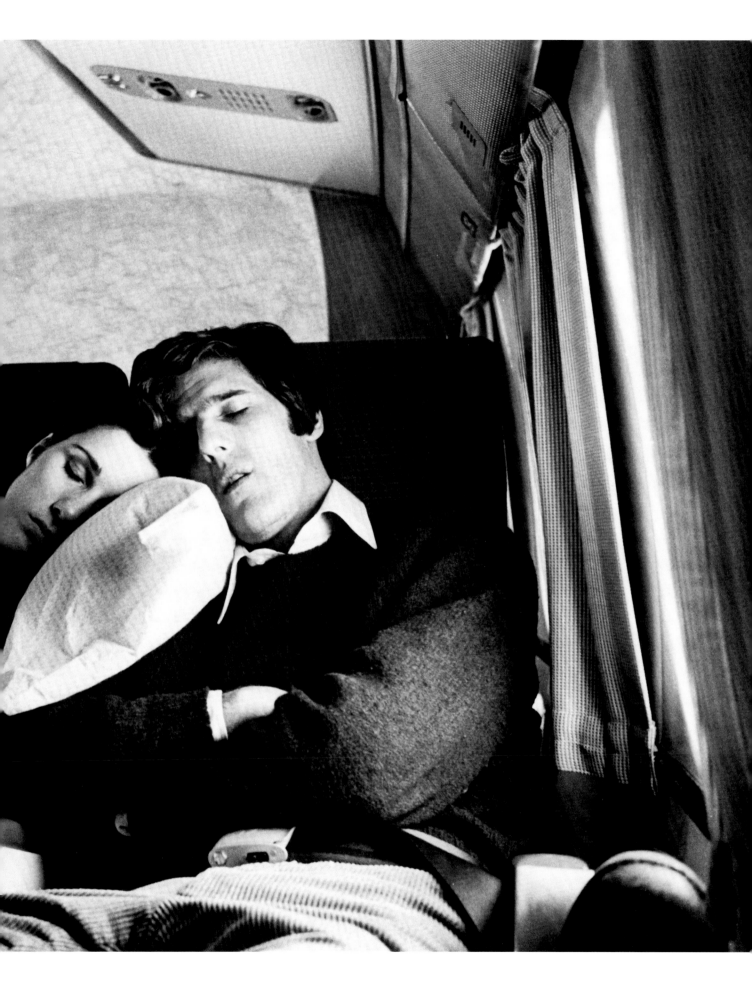

Democratic National Convention

Miami, Florida, July 10, 1972

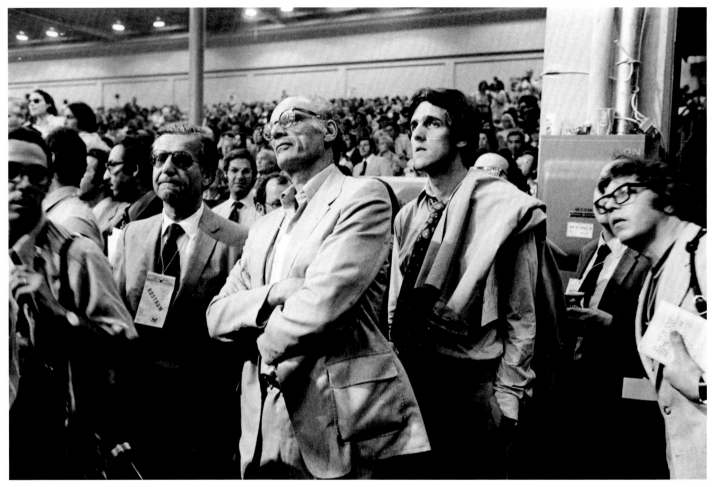

Arthur Miller (center), John Kerry, Pete Hamill.

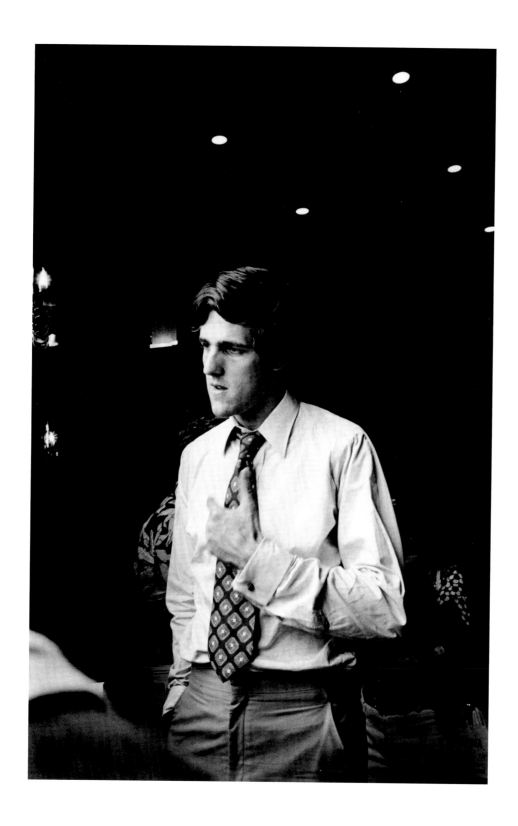

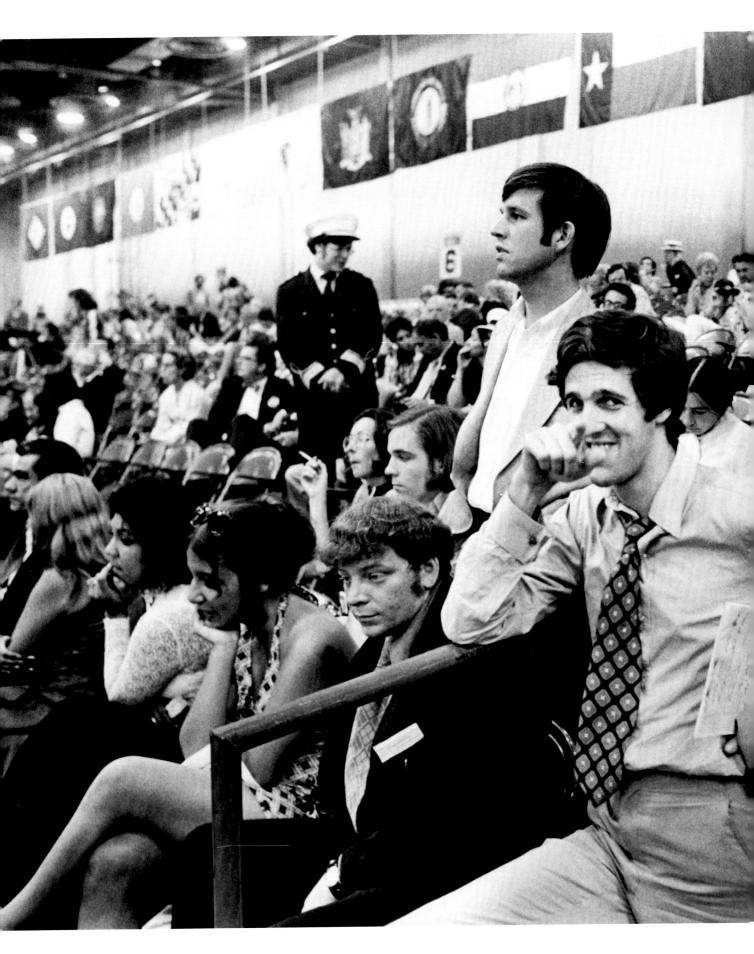

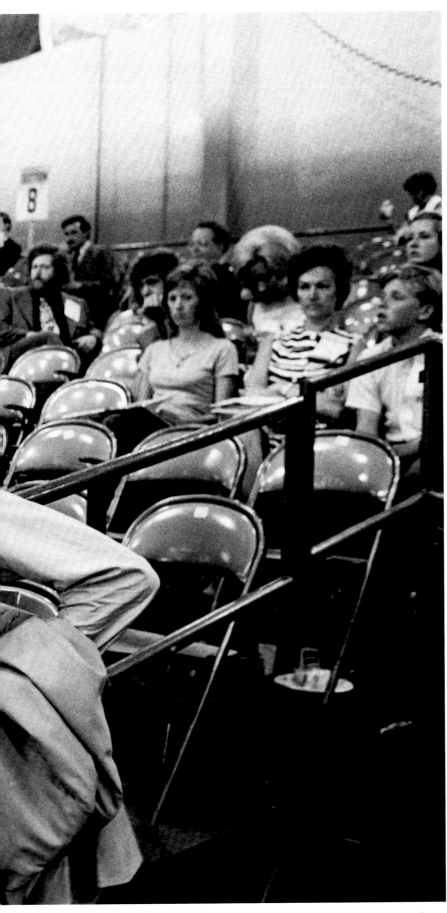

Democratic National Convention, Miami, Florida, 1972.
A rare moment when John had time to acknowledge my Leica.

John Kerry Enters the Race for Congress in the Fifth Massachusetts District

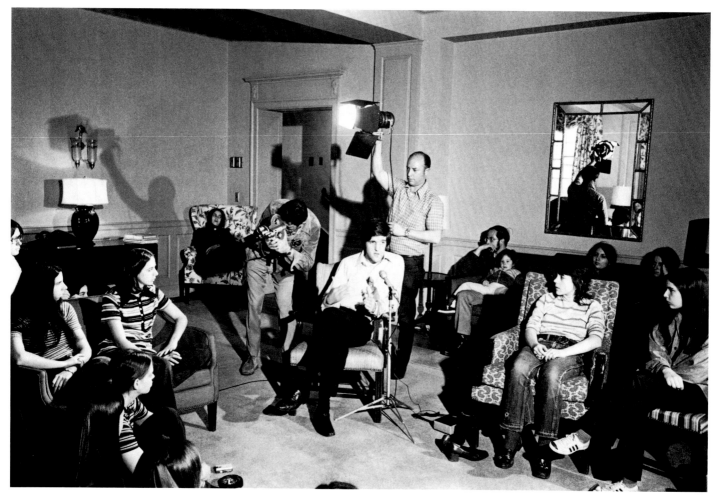

John addresses students in Andover, Massachusetts, April 1972.

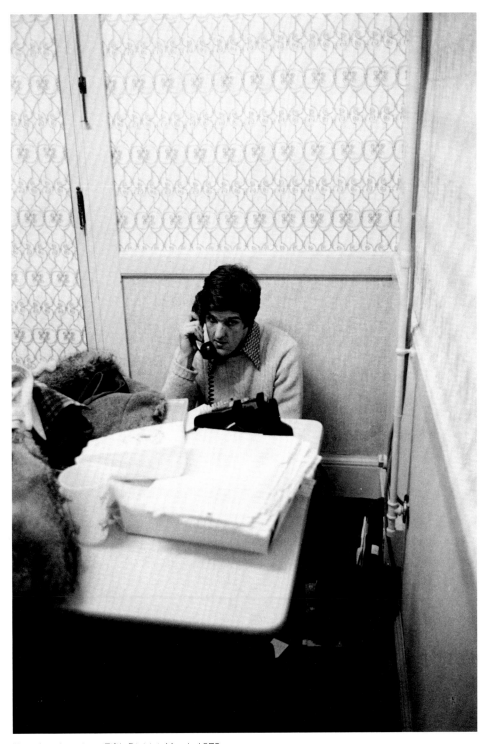

Kerry headquarters, Fifth District, March 1972.

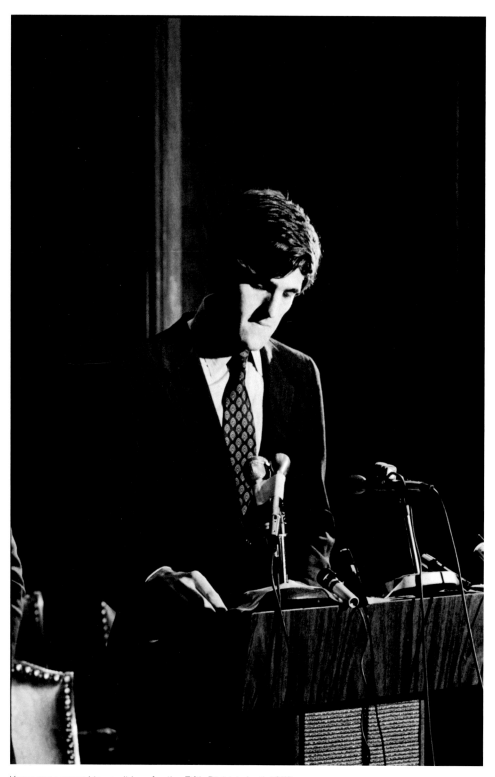

Kerry announces his candidacy for the Fifth District, April 1972.

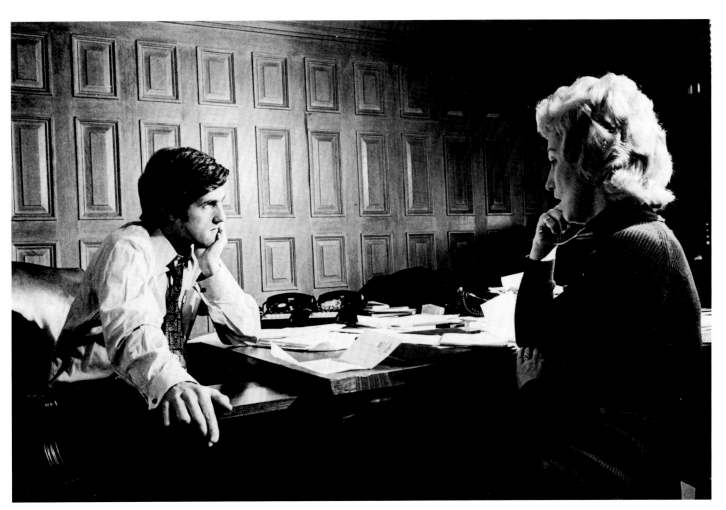

Virginia Sherwood, an ABC correspondent, interviews John at campaign headquarters.

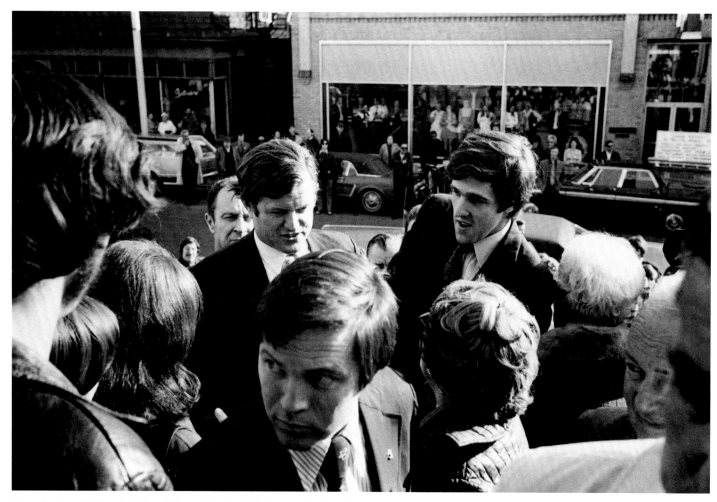

Campaigning with Senator Edward Kennedy in the Fifth District, October 1972.

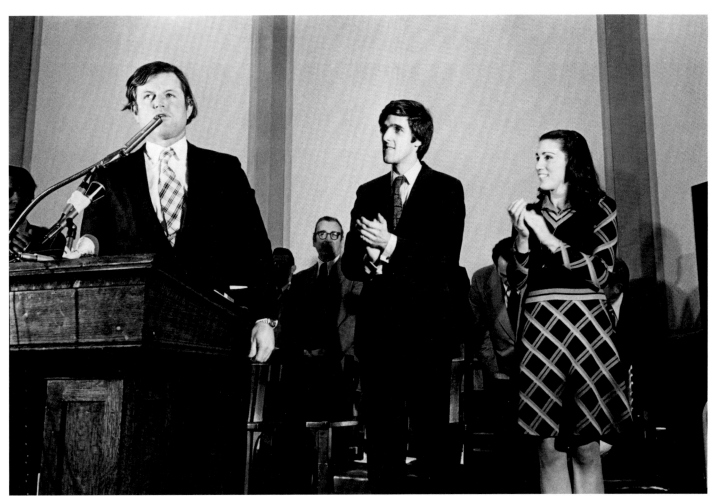

John, who got his start in grassroots politics volunteering for Senator Kennedy's first campaign in 1962, begins to forge a lifelong relationship with Teddy. Shortly before this picture was taken, I was sitting next to an open seat on a shuttle from Washington to Boston. As the doors shut, a burly figure appeared at my side and Senator Kennedy took the seat. During the flight I brought up John. "My goodness, he's doing well," said the Senator. "I've never seen anyone so young do so well."

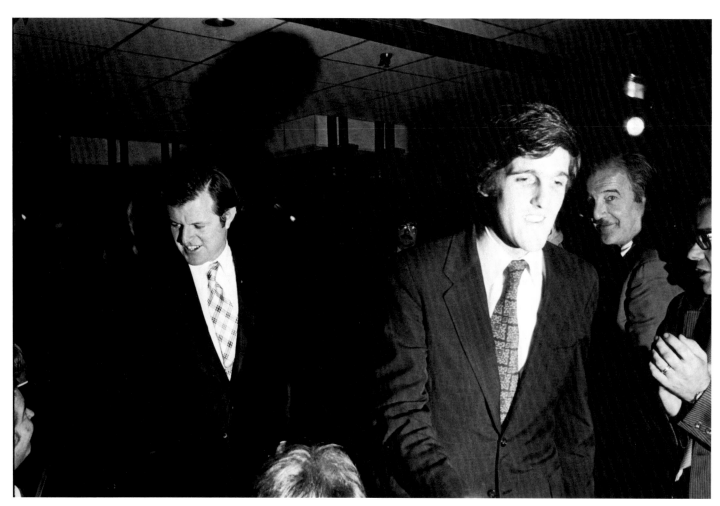

Ted Kennedy and John Kerry, Lowell, Massachusetts, October 1972.

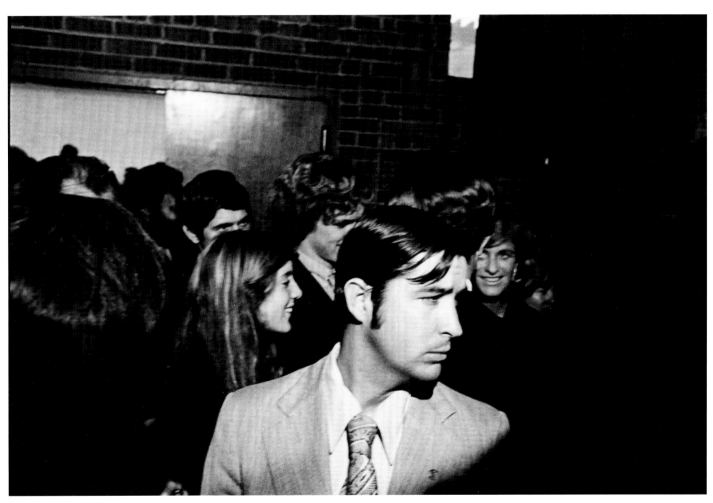

Caroline and Joe Kennedy III, at Kerry rally, Fifth District, April 1972. A security gaurd is in the foreground.

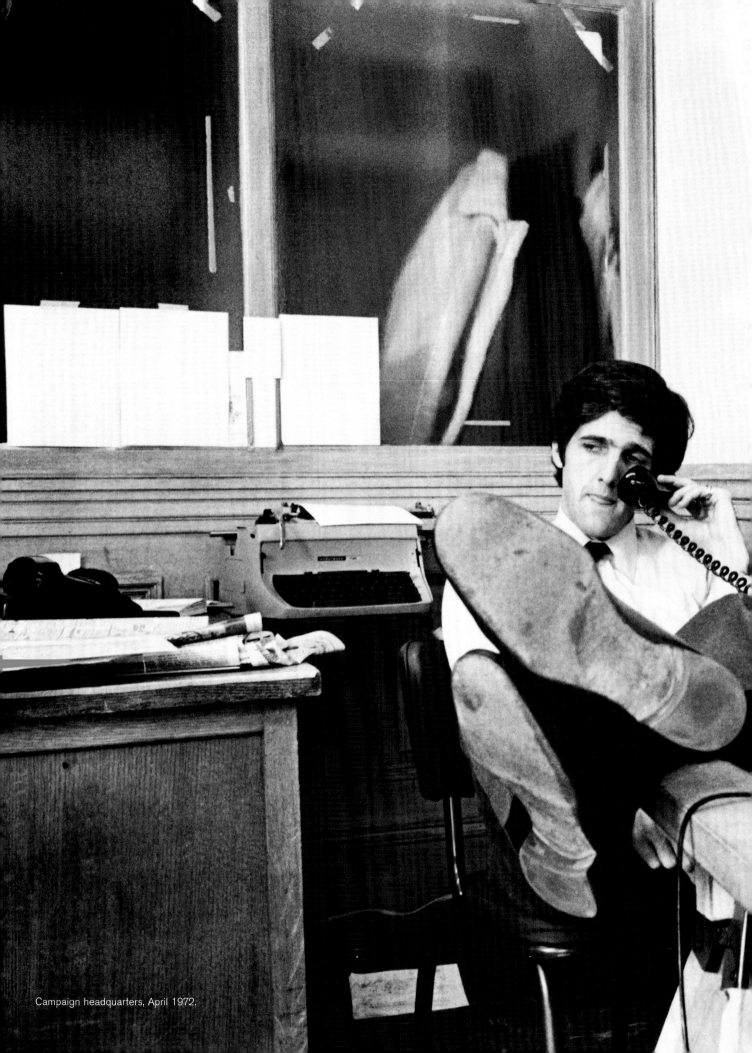

Campaign headquarters, April 1972.

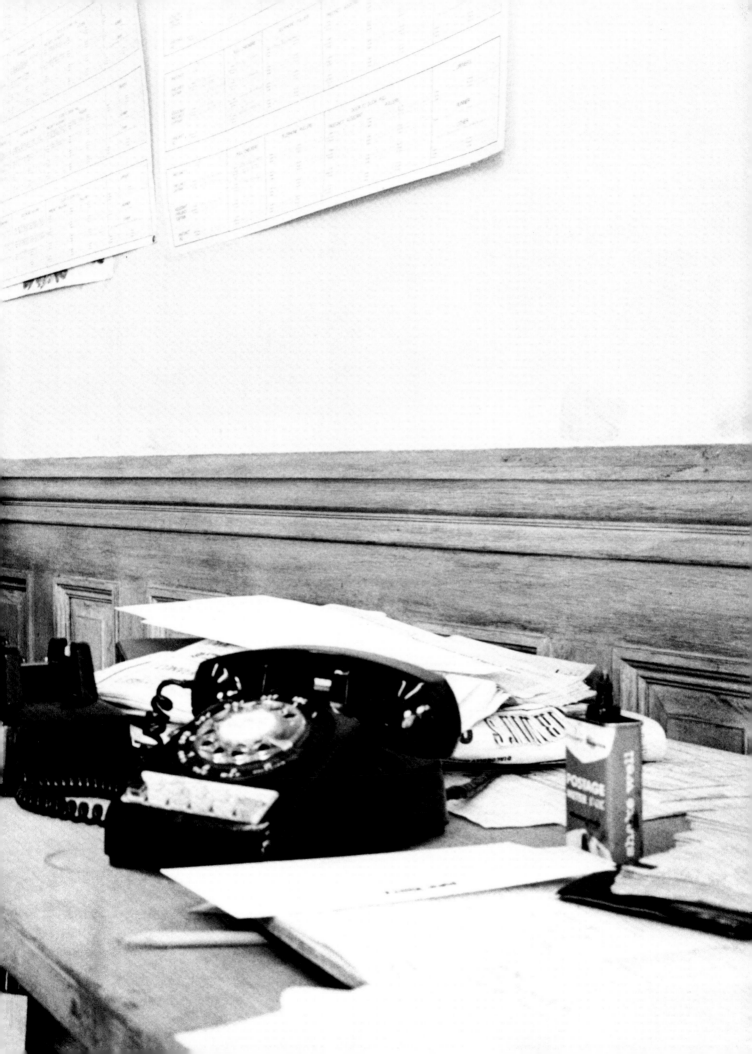

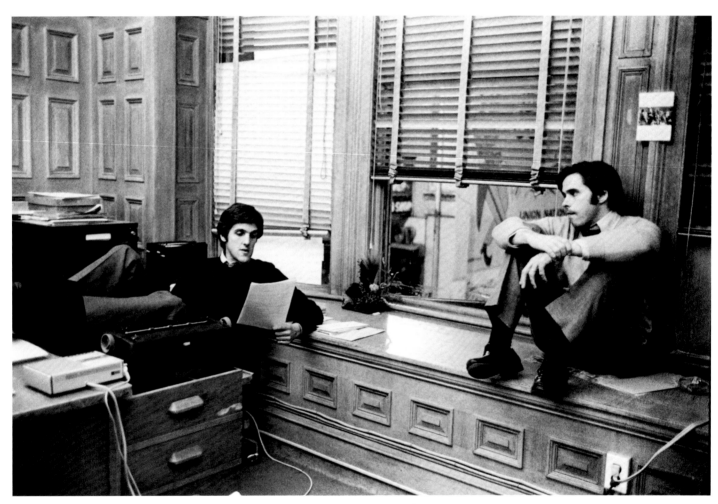

John and campaign adviser David Thorne, campaign headquarters, Fifth District, March 1972.

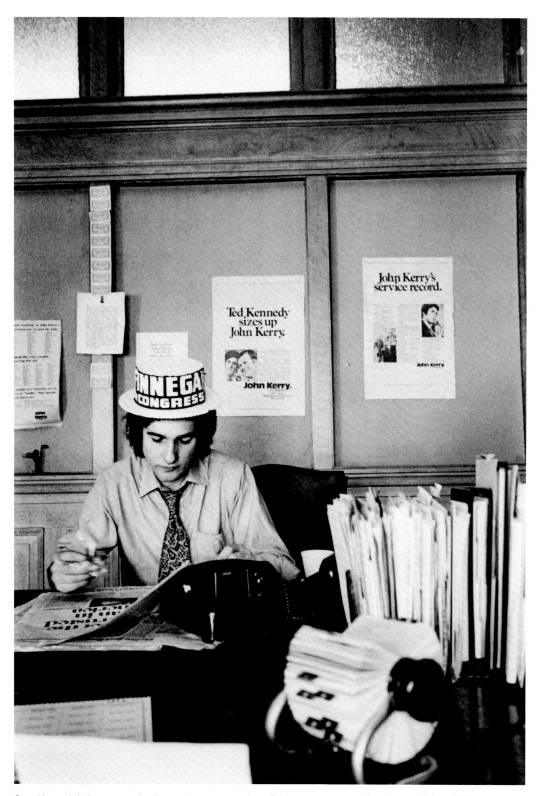

Cam Kerry, John's younger brother and an important confidant, campaign headquarters, October 1972.

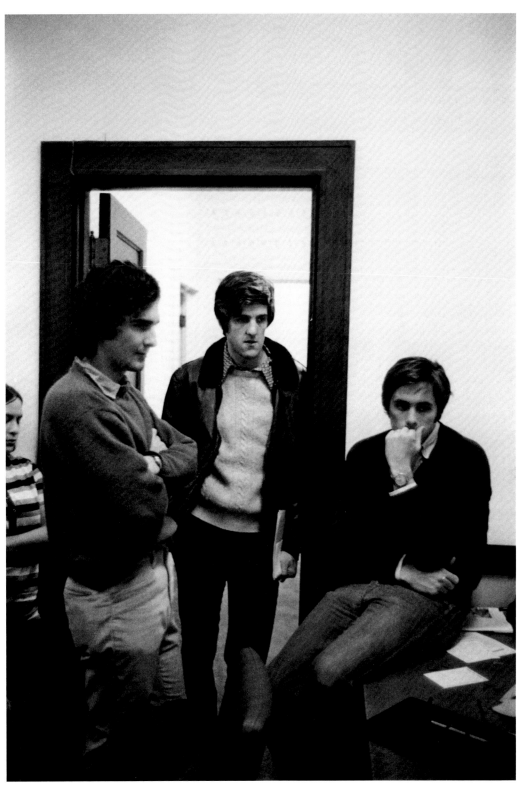

Kerry flanked by Cam and David Thorne, his closest advisers, April 1972.

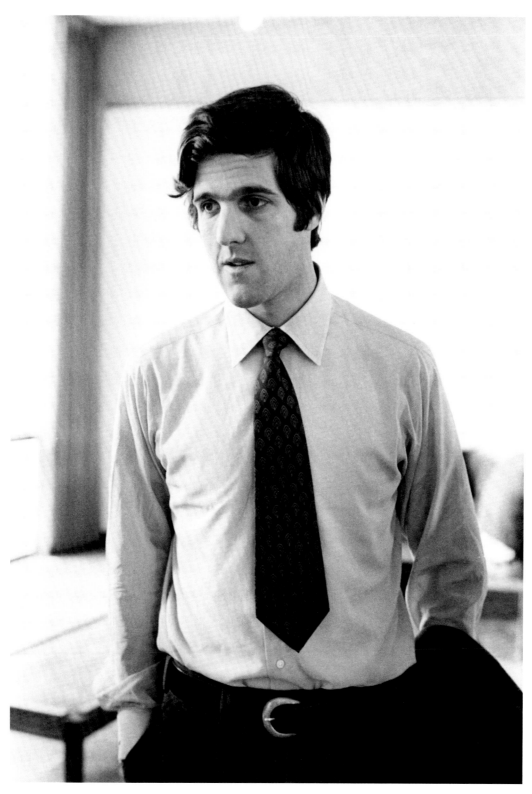

John in April 1972.

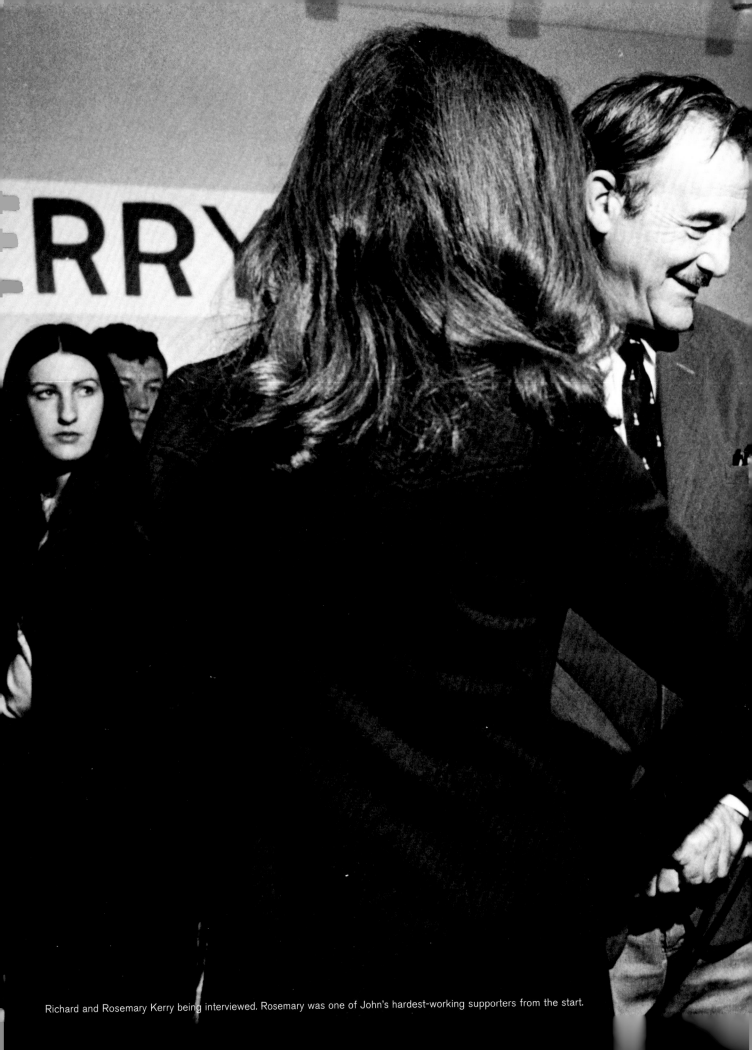

Richard and Rosemary Kerry being interviewed. Rosemary was one of John's hardest-working supporters from the start.

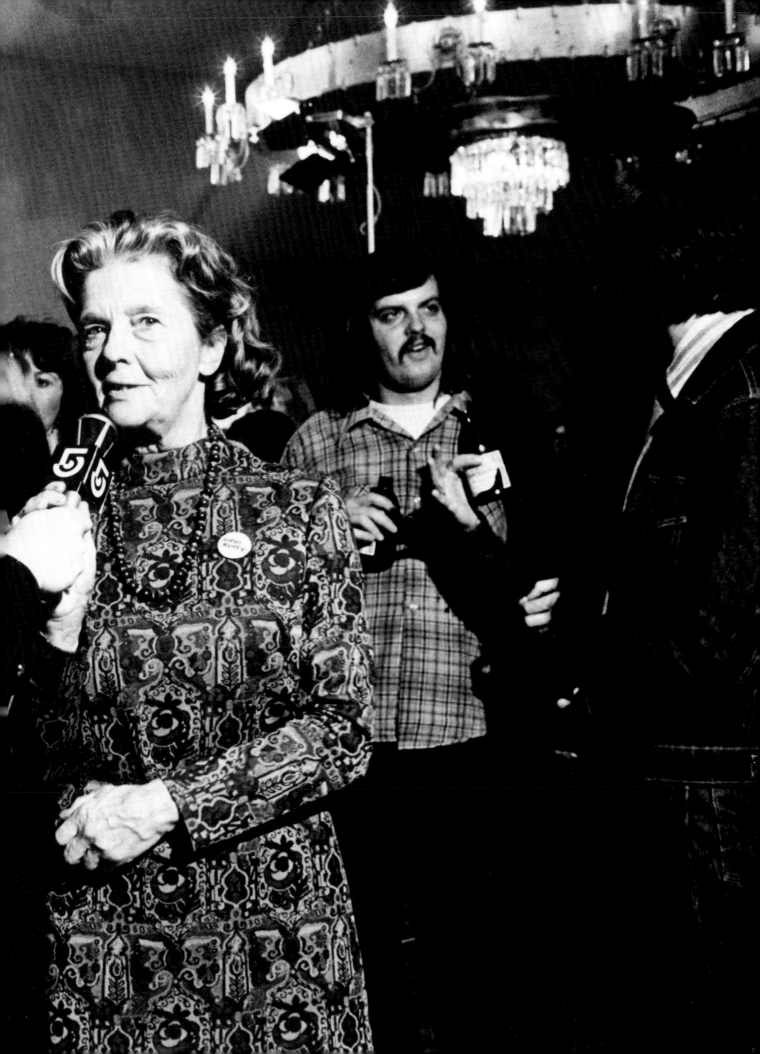

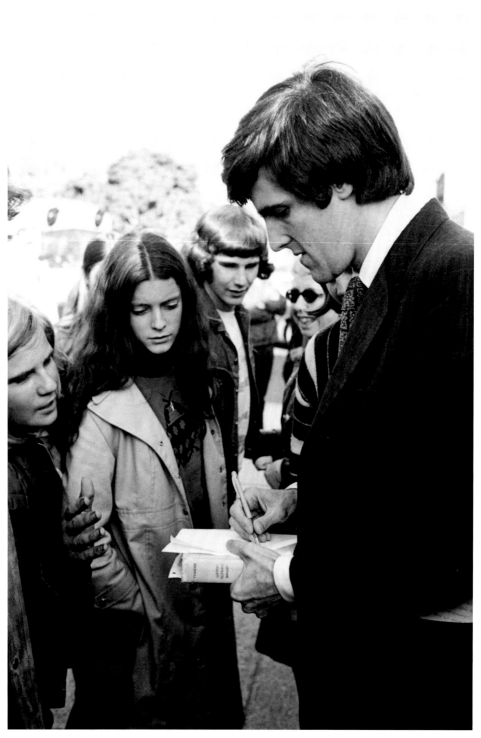

Campaigning in the Fifth District, October 1972.

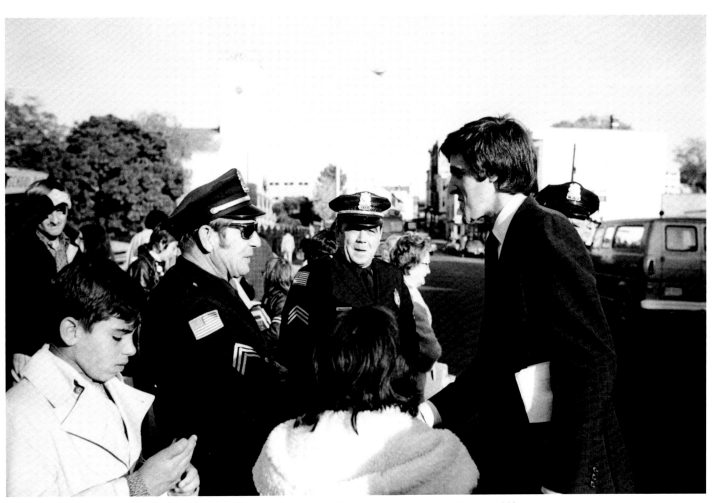

John had a natural shyness, but he threw himself into campaigning — and became quite good at it. October 1972.

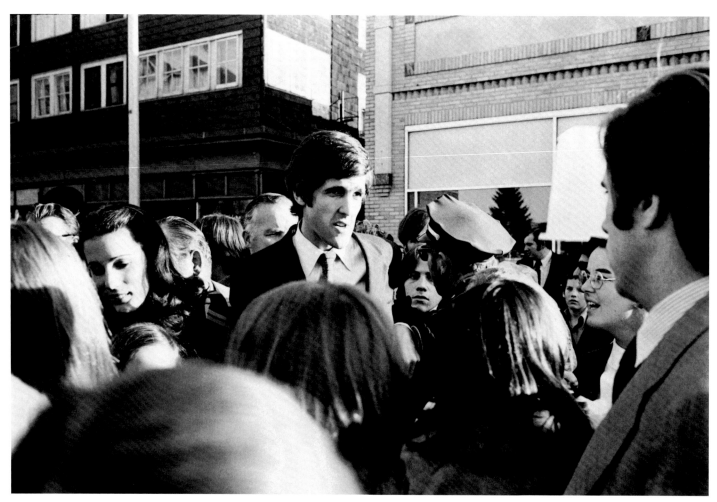

An apocryphal story grew up around the 1972 campaign. To wit, John put in such long hours that his driver, who came to pick up the candidate in the dark hours of one morning, could get no response to the doorbell. Concerned, he entered John's house — and found him asleep in the shower.

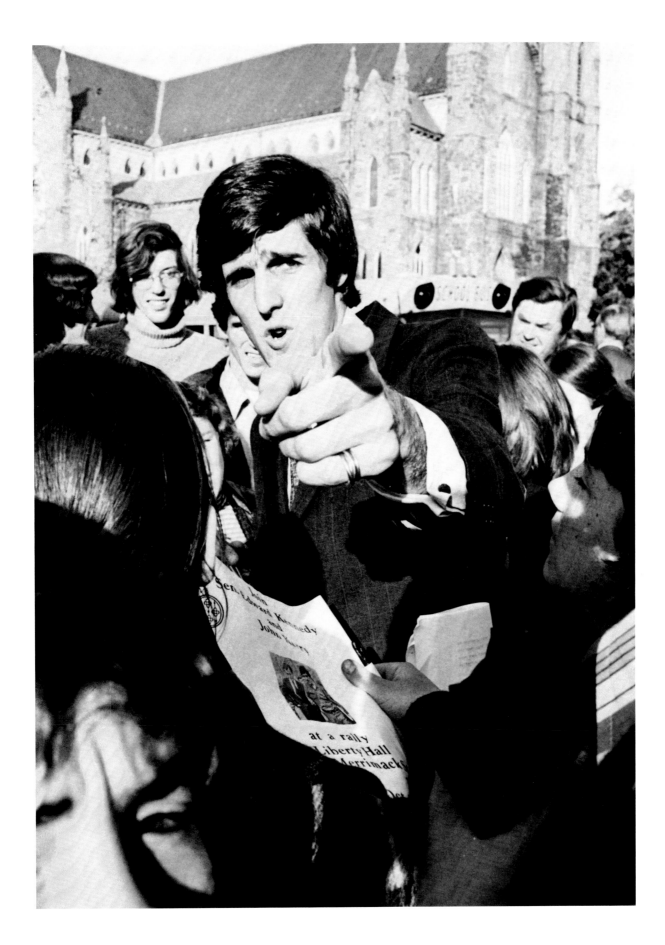

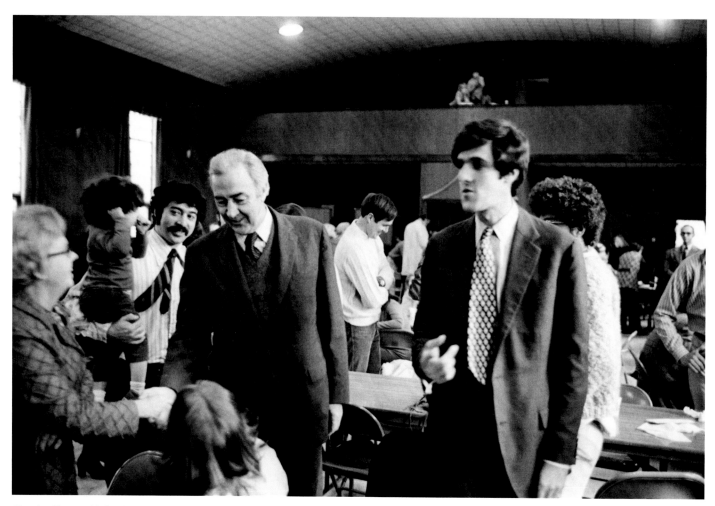

Senator Eugene McCarthy campaigns for Kerry.

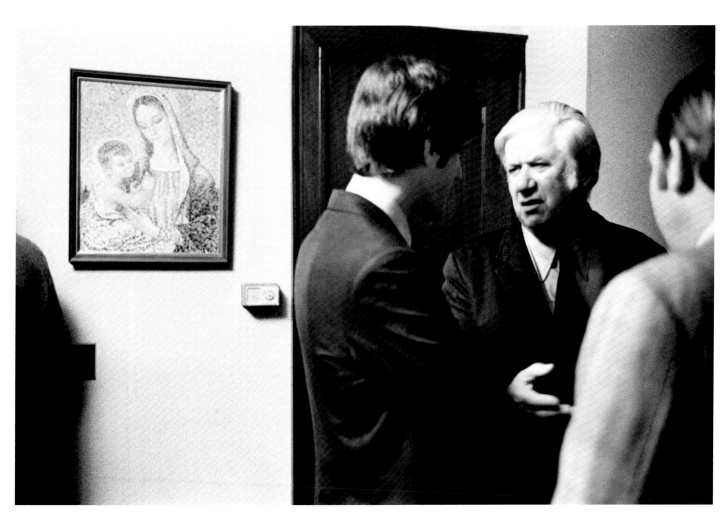

"Tip" O'Neill, Speaker of the House, at a fund-raiser for Kerry, October 1972.

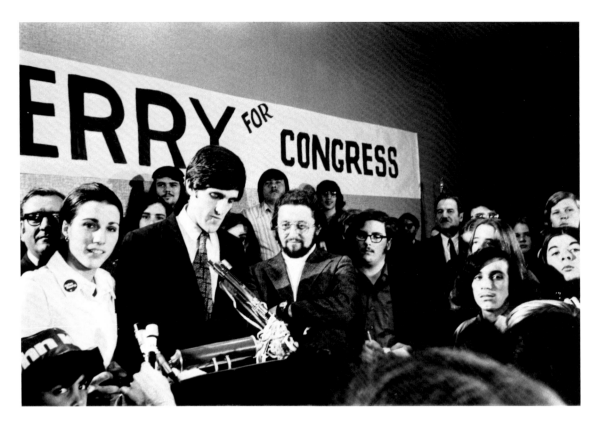

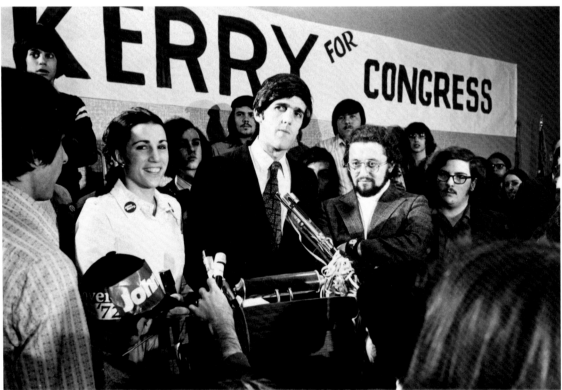

Having won the primary against seven Democrats, Kerry fell under heavy political attack — probably orchestrated by the Nixon White House — and he lost the election. These photographs are of his concession speech on the evening of November 2, 1972.

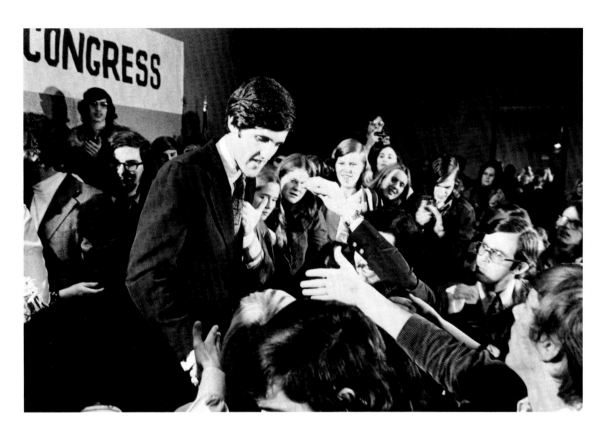

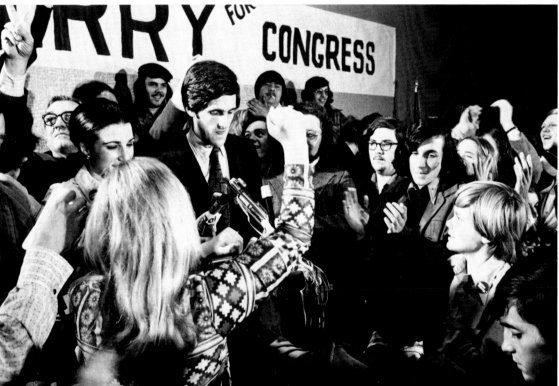

Losing this race the way he did was a surprise. He'd never seen his character questioned. Kerry said in his concession speech: "We came together over an idea — that the war in Vietnam, which is not over, should be. If I had to do it again, I'd be in Washington with the veterans tomorrow."

As he left the room, I followed him. He turned and said, "George, I believe I was correct." He repeated himself: "Very correct." Then he was gone.

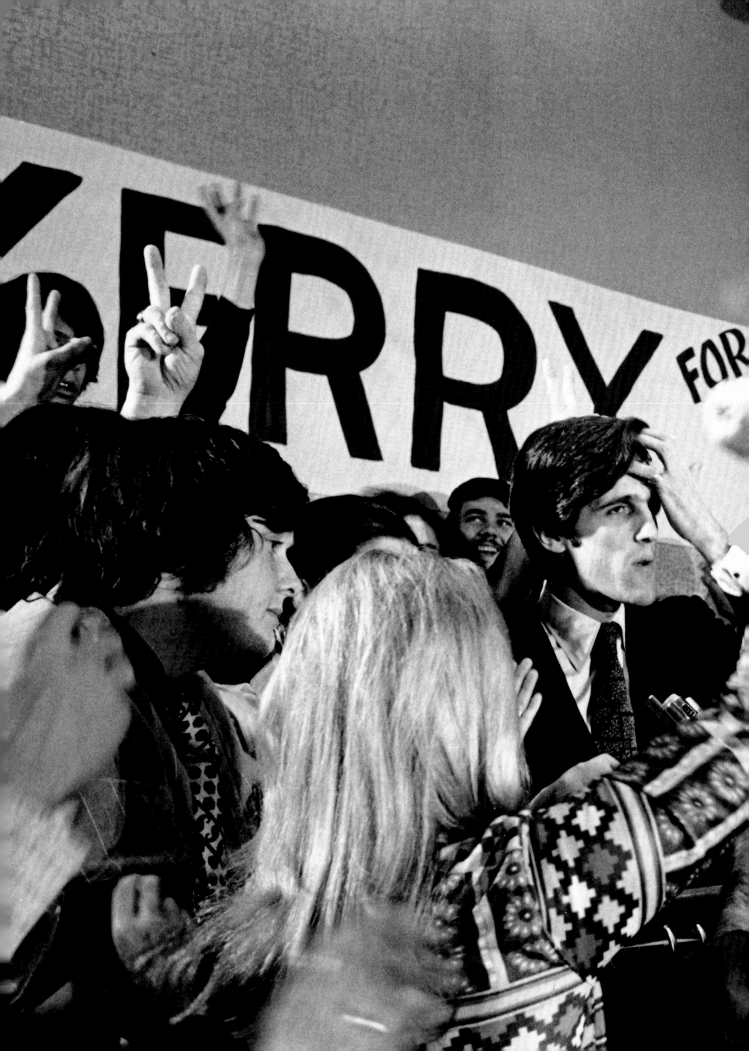

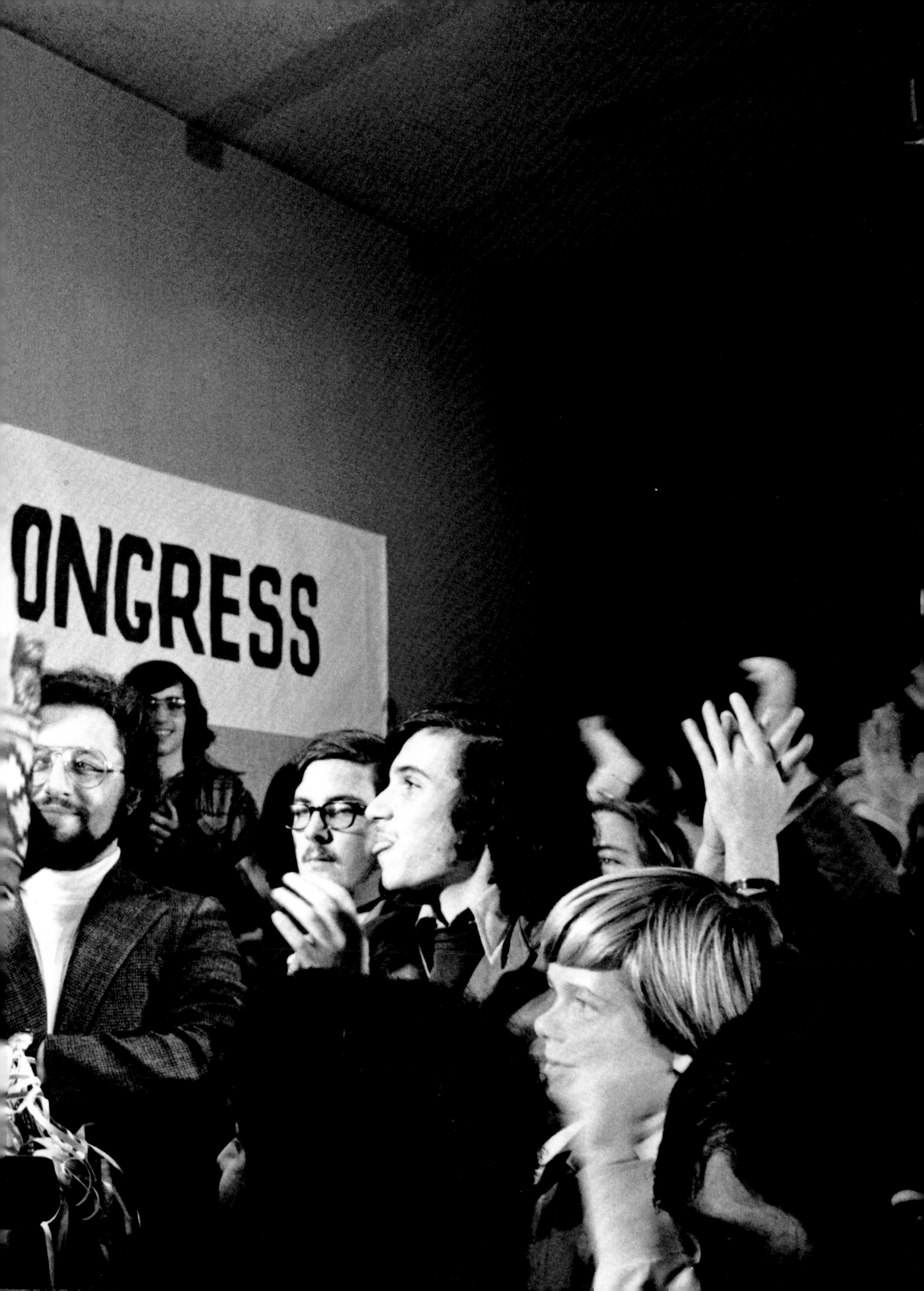
ONGRESS

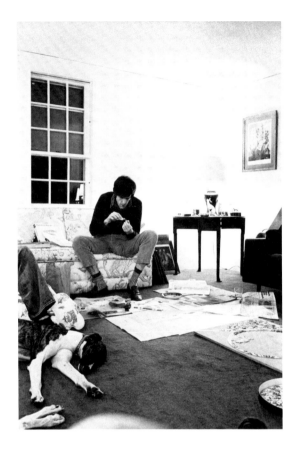

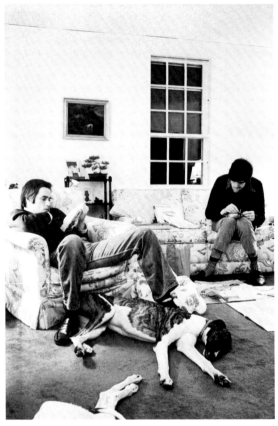

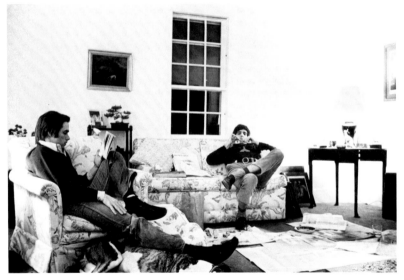

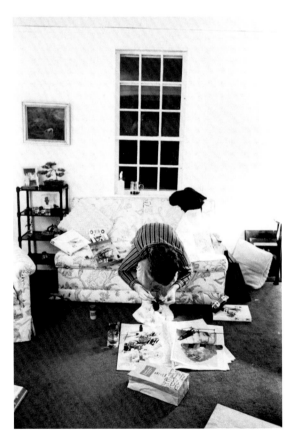

After his election-night defeat, John and Julia came up to my farm in New Hampshire for some quiet. John was quiet and reflective during his visit. After months of nonstop campaigning, he returned to a hobby his father had shared with him, meditatively assembling a number of model planes and ships as David Thorne read and my dogs slept. He was stunned by the fierce negative attacks that had been launched against him. It had shaken his whole idea of how politics was supposed to work. We wondered what he'd do next.

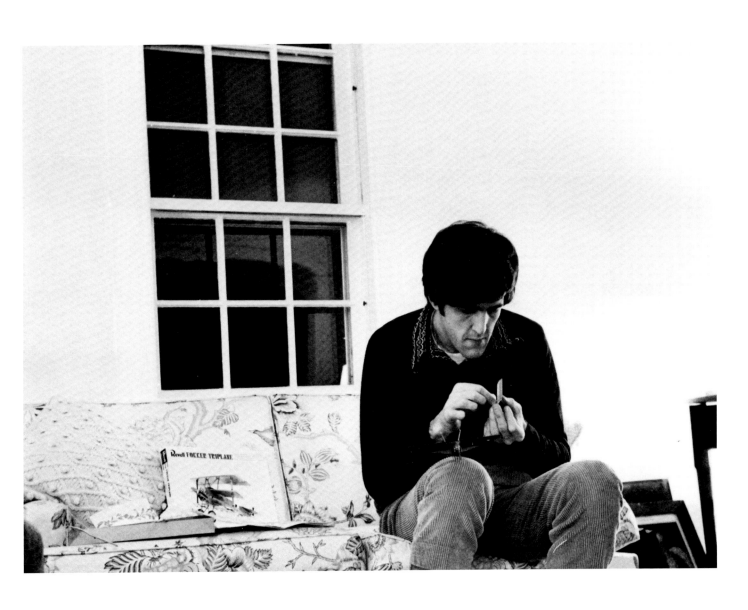

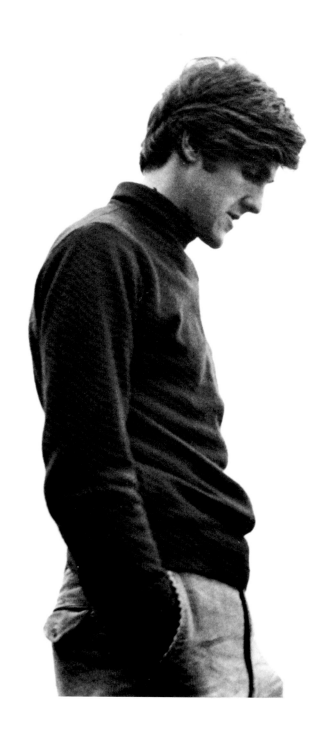

The day after the election was cold and rainy. I took John up Mt. Webster. He wasn't talking much. He just looked down through the fog, trying to make sense of what had happened and how he had been tested. This was a signal moment. A lesser man might have given up politics and switched to an easier career.

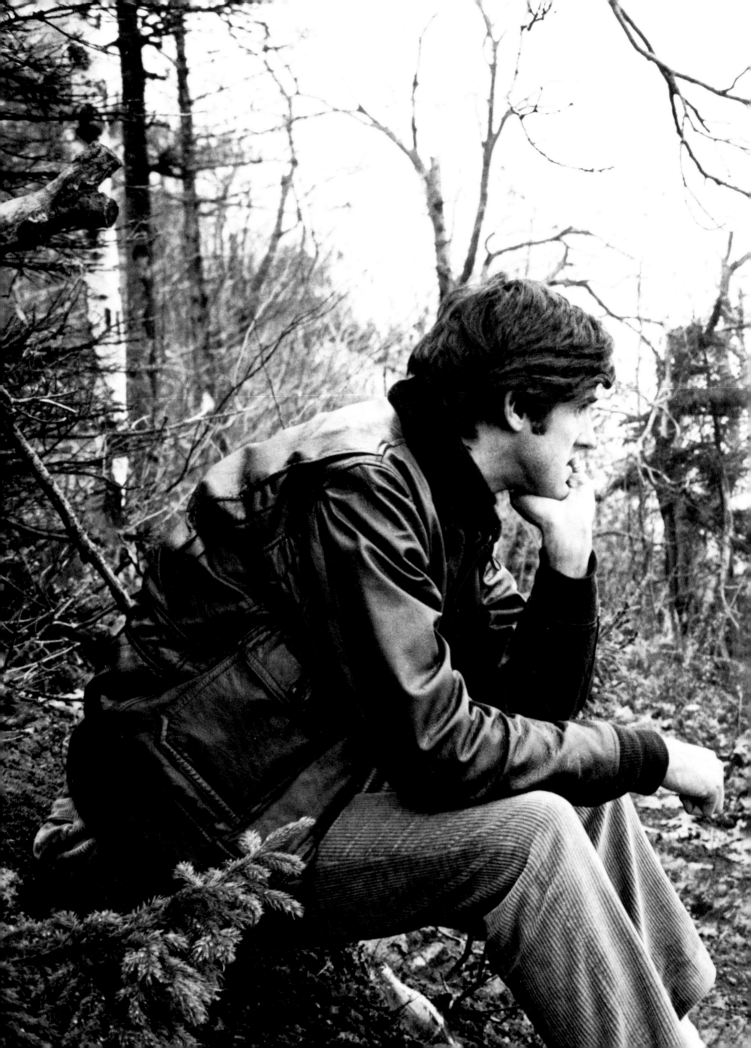

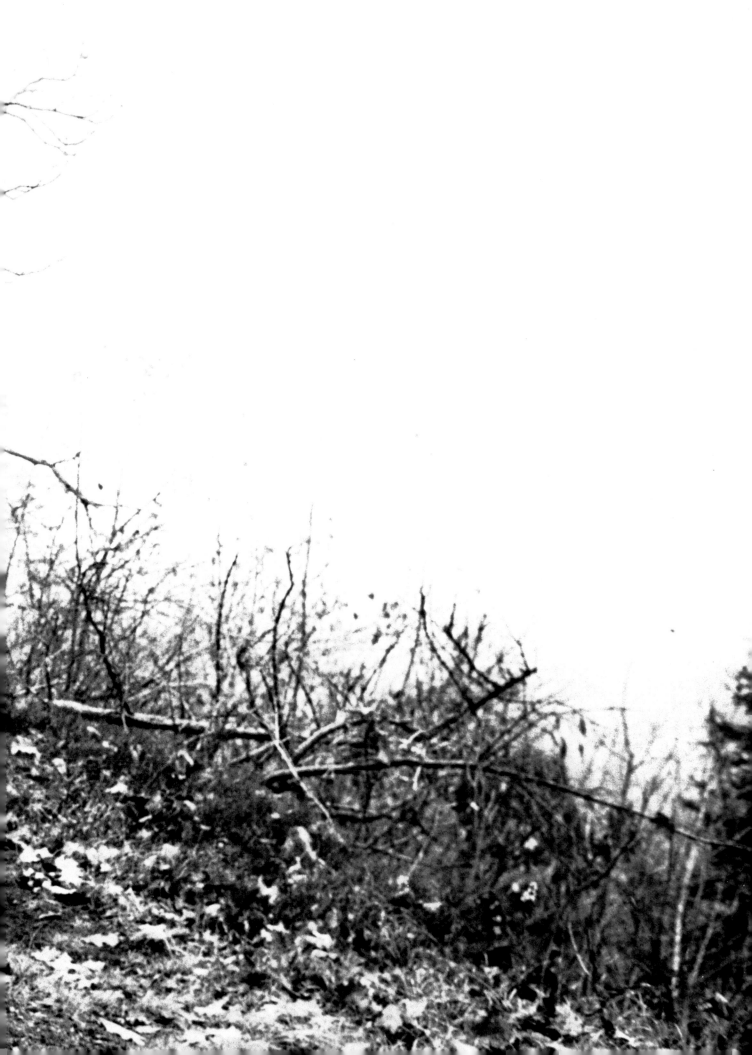

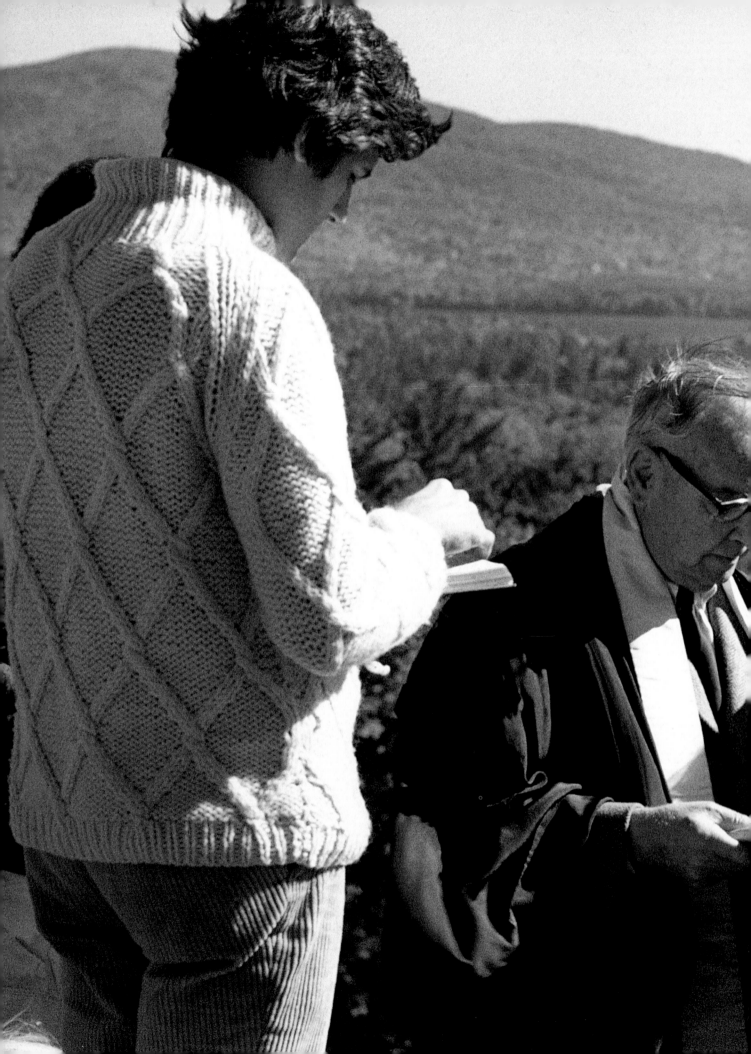

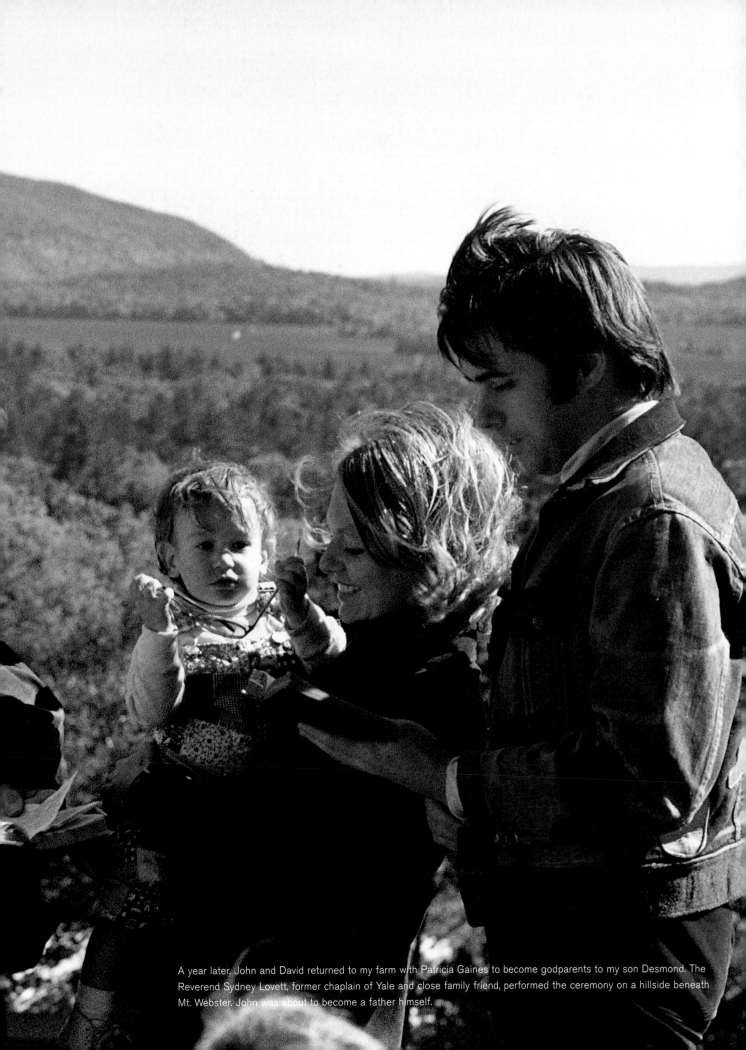

A year later, John and David returned to my farm with Patricia Gaines to become godparents to my son Desmond. The Reverend Sydney Lovett, former chaplain of Yale and close family friend, performed the ceremony on a hillside beneath Mt. Webster. John was about to become a father himself.

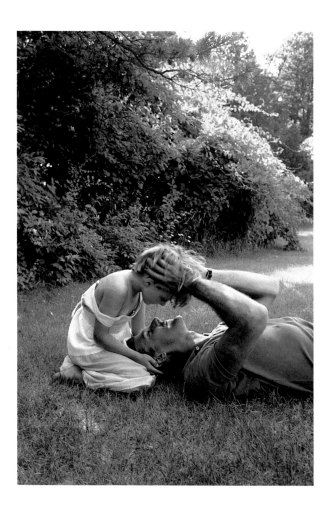

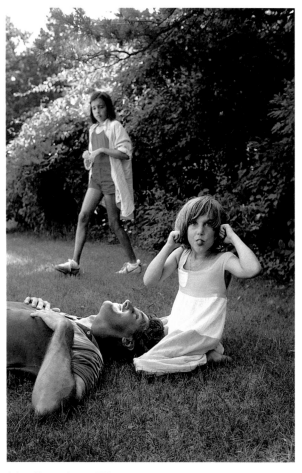

John, Alexendra, and Vanessa.

John and his daughters, Vanessa and Alexandra, August 1982.

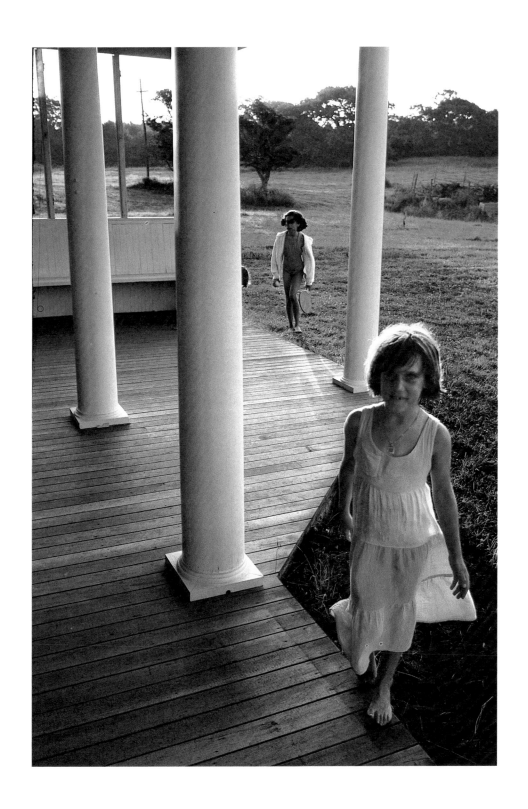

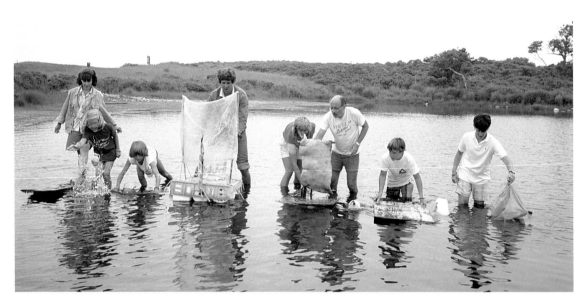

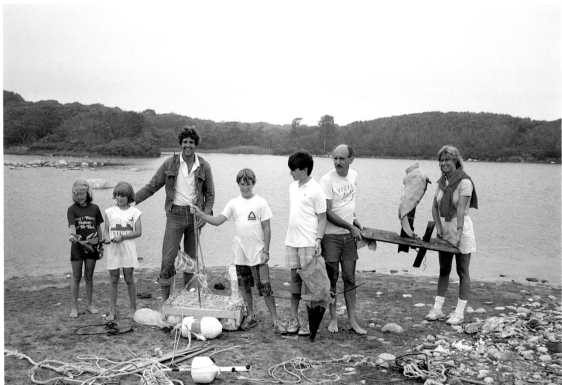

Here is a curious game for children, but a useful one. Kerry bewailed the amount of trash on beaches, so he challenged all our children to make sailboats out of washed-up trash. Then there was an elaborate race. He offered an award to the winner. But his "boat" — with the biggest sail — won.

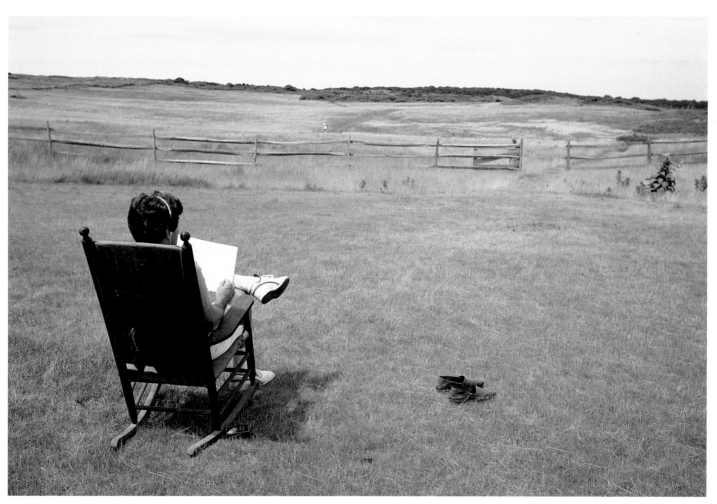

On a clear summer day, with a good sea breeze, John Kerry draws on his sketch pad.

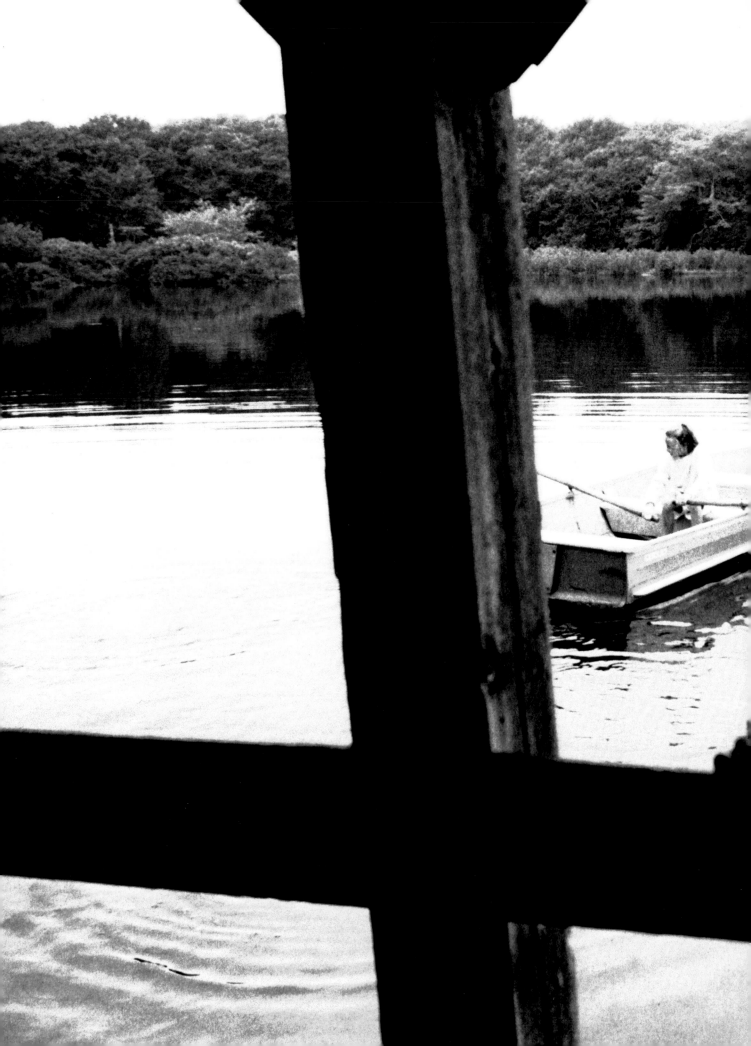

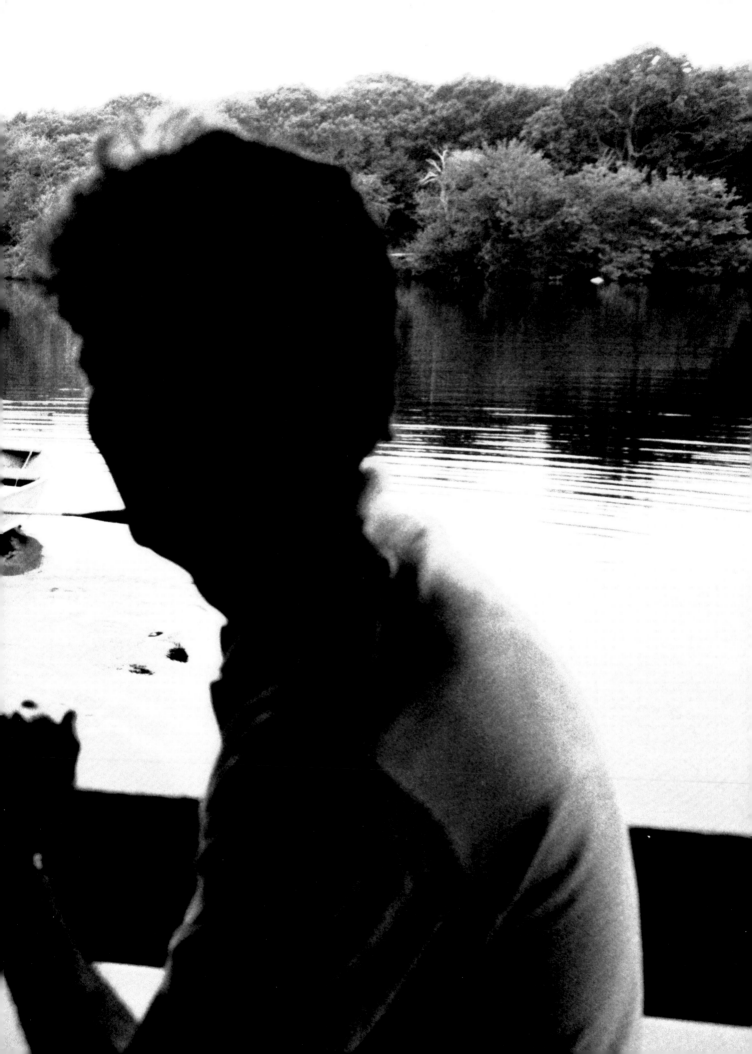

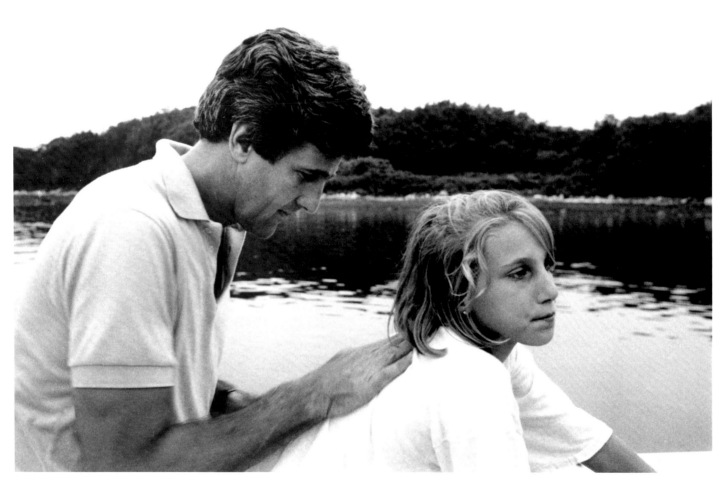

John and Vanessa, July 1987.

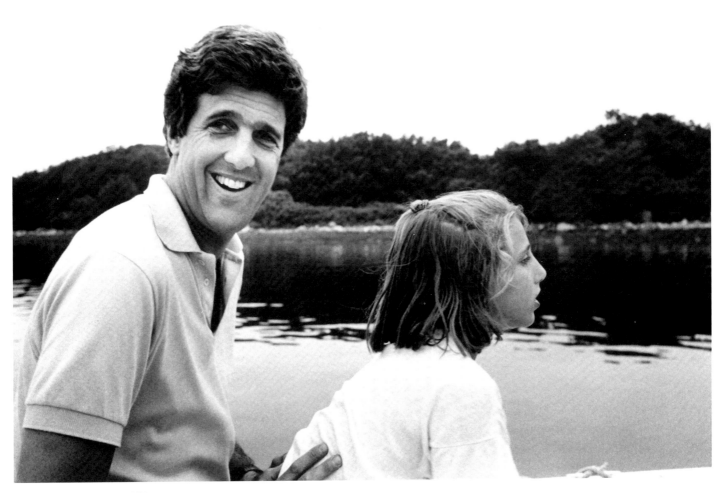

Vanessa and John, July 1987.

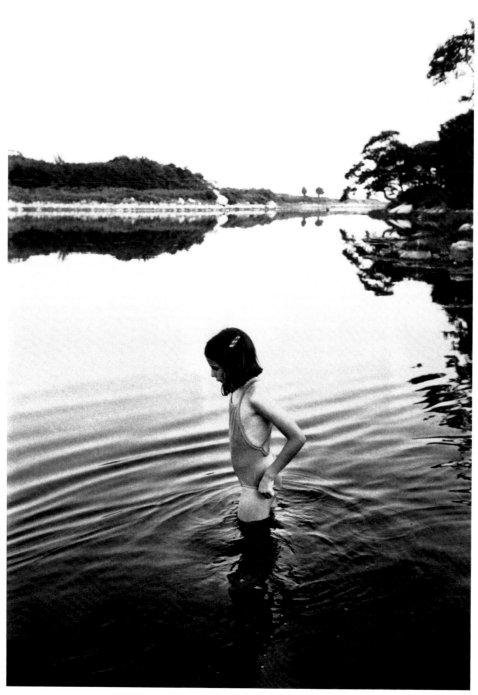

Alex Kerry, July 1983.

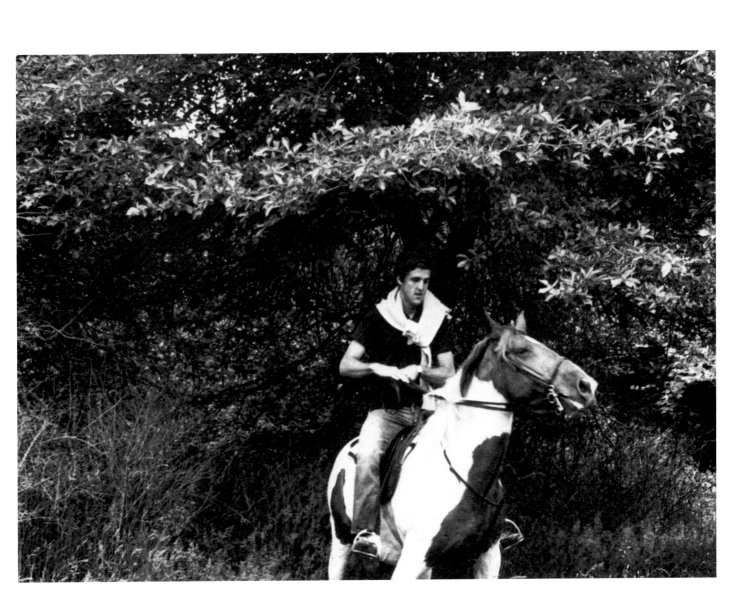

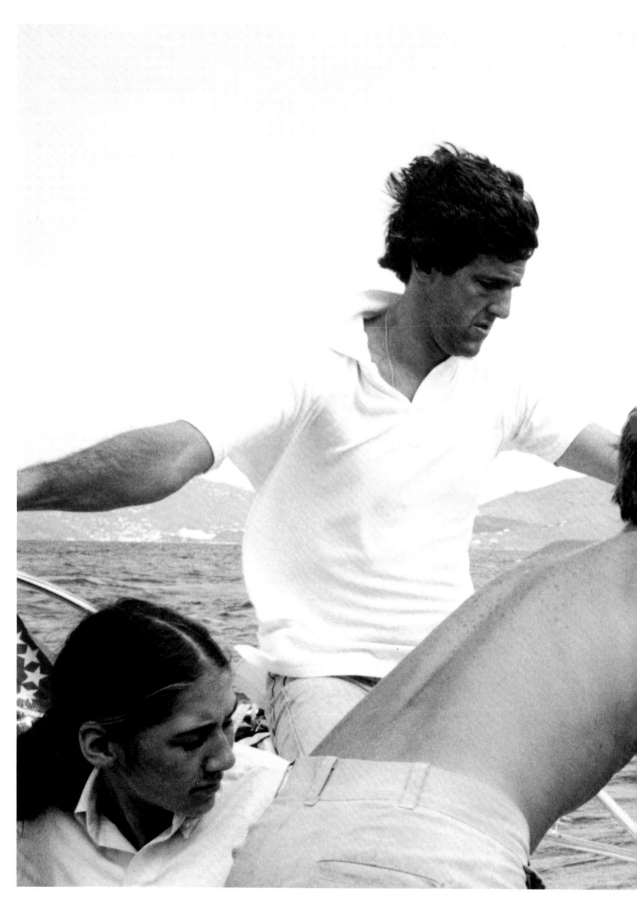

Sailing, March 1983. John was helmsman and navigator. These skills led him to join the Navy in 1966.
At every opportunity, he goes back to the water.

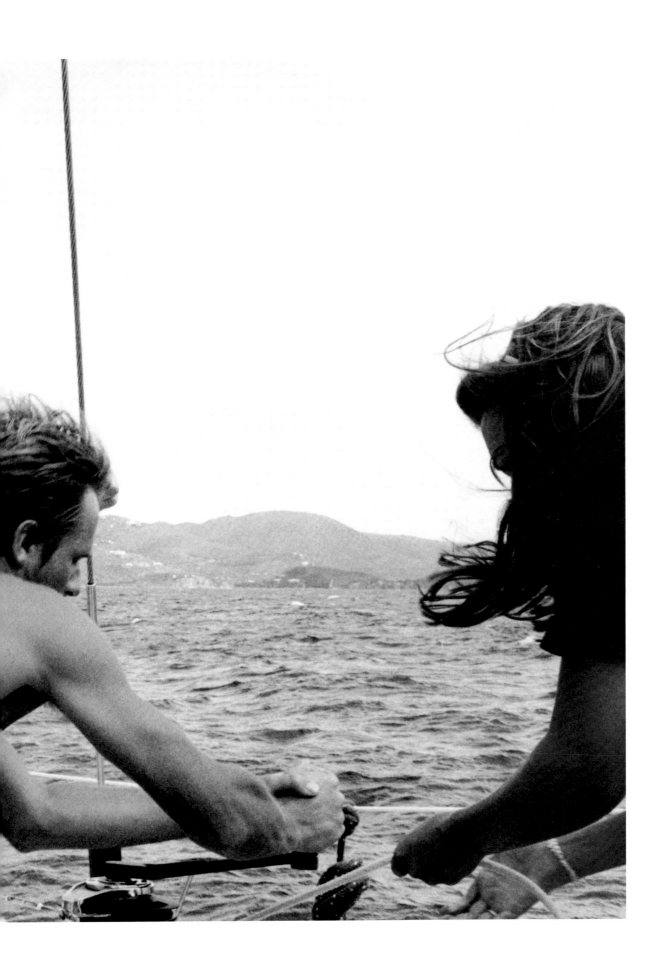

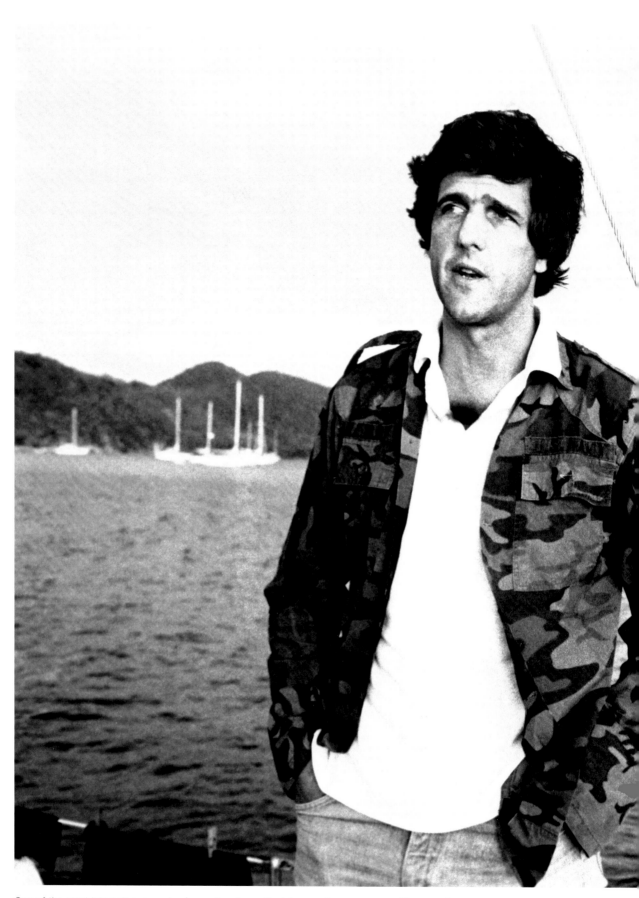

One of the most interesting aspects of spending time with John was the awareness of how much was racing through his mind. He spent his downtime thinking. March 1983.

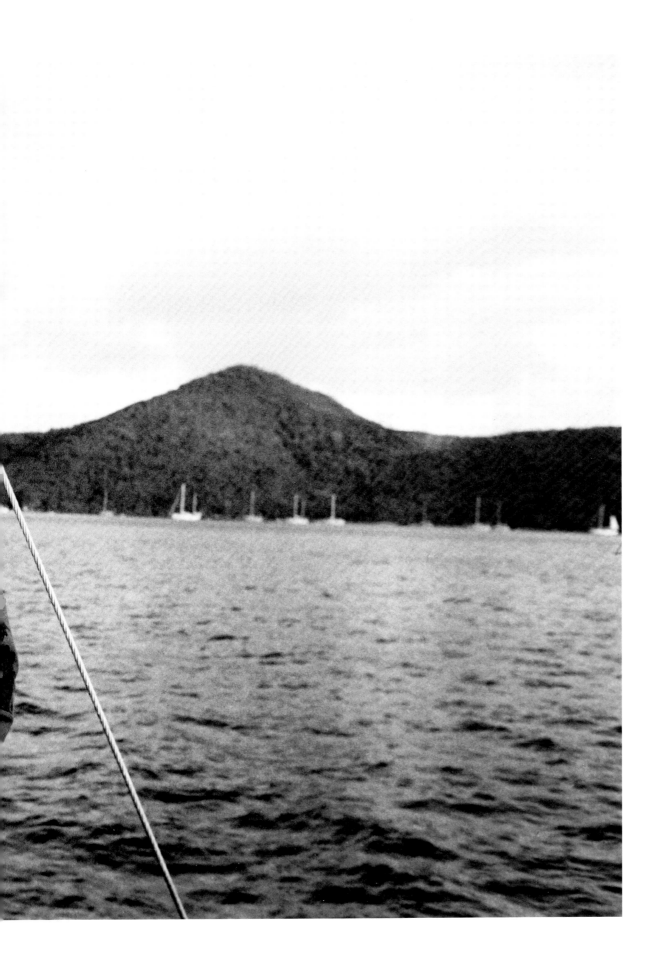

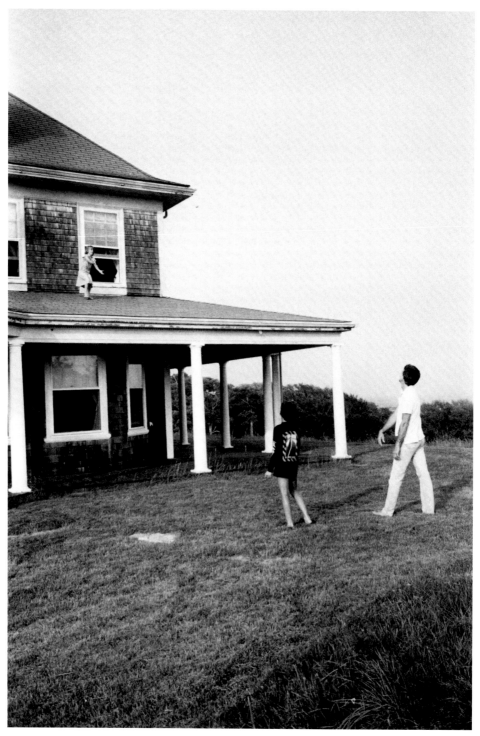

My son Desmond, Vanessa, and John playing roof ball, July 1984.

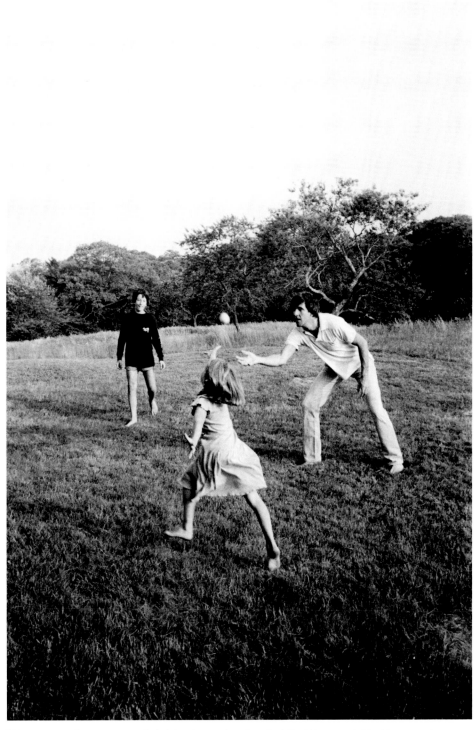

This was one of many games that John dreamed up for all of the kids around. The idea was, always be active.

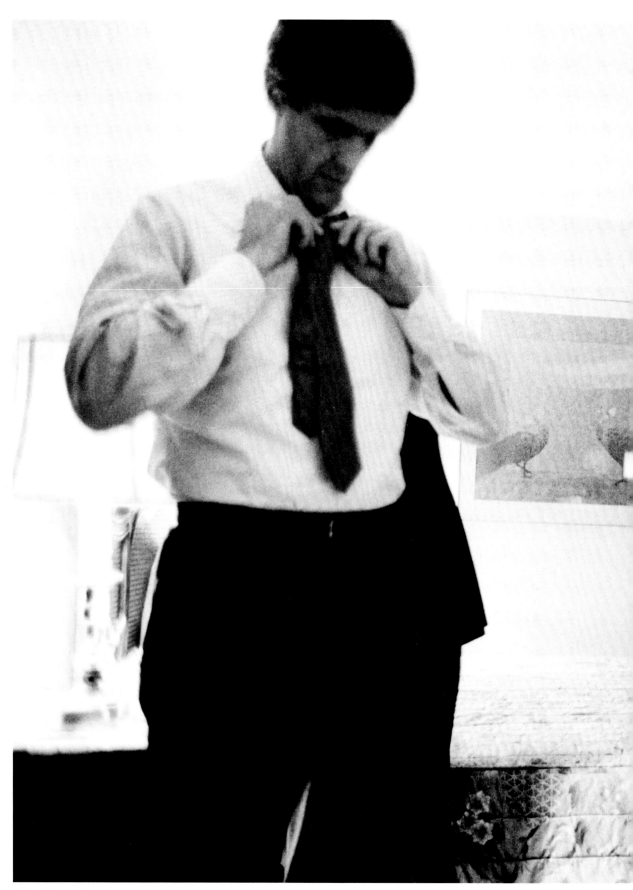

John, Alex, and Vanessa in a hotel room hours before victory in the 1984 Senate race, Boston, Massachusetts.

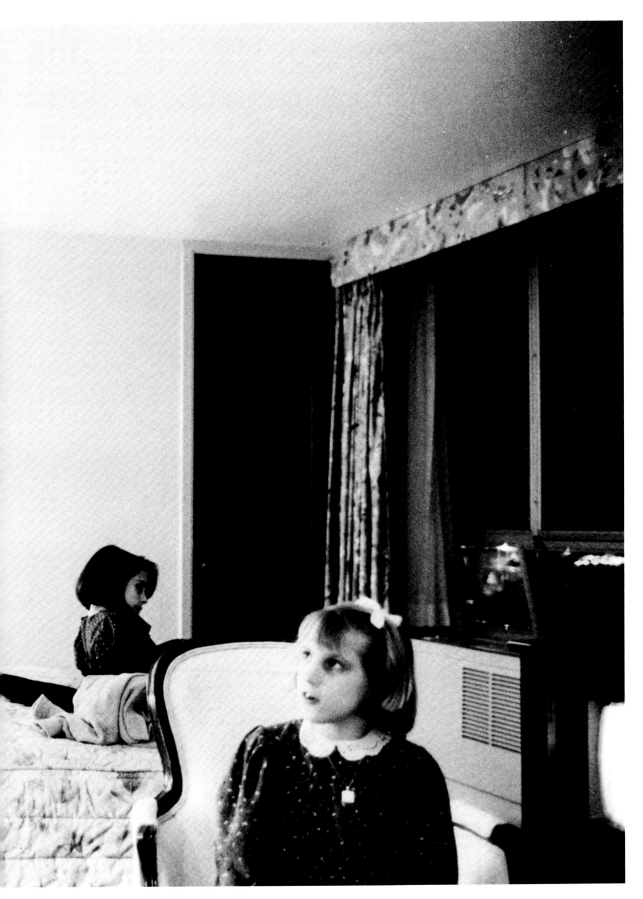

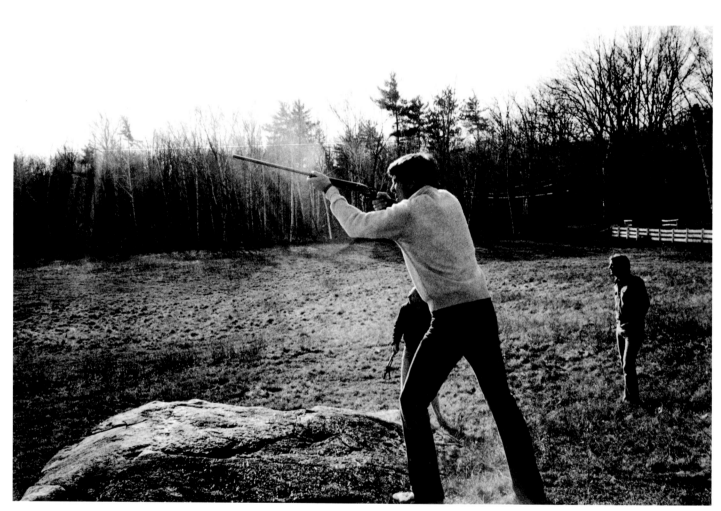

Shooting clay pigeons in Holderness, New Hampshire, Thanksgiving 1984.

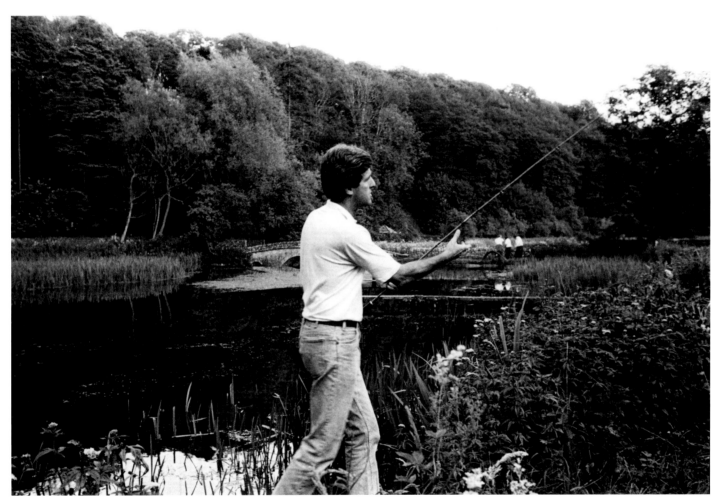

Fishing, August 1987.

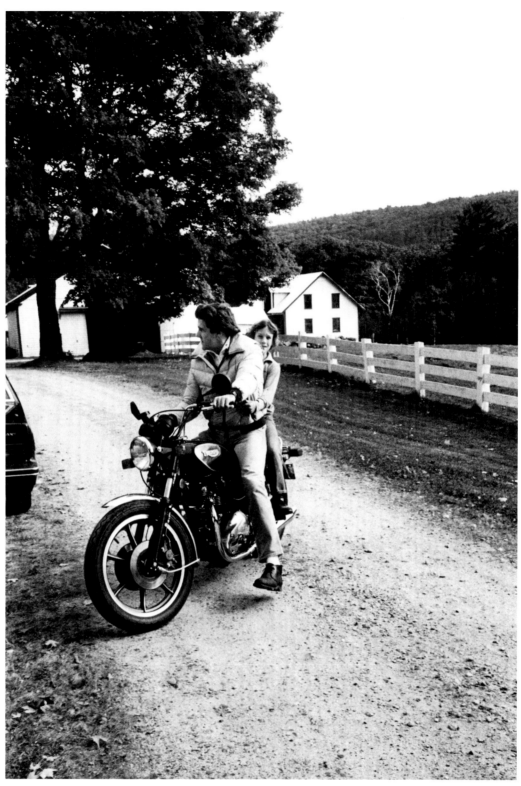

John and my son Tyssen, September 1983.

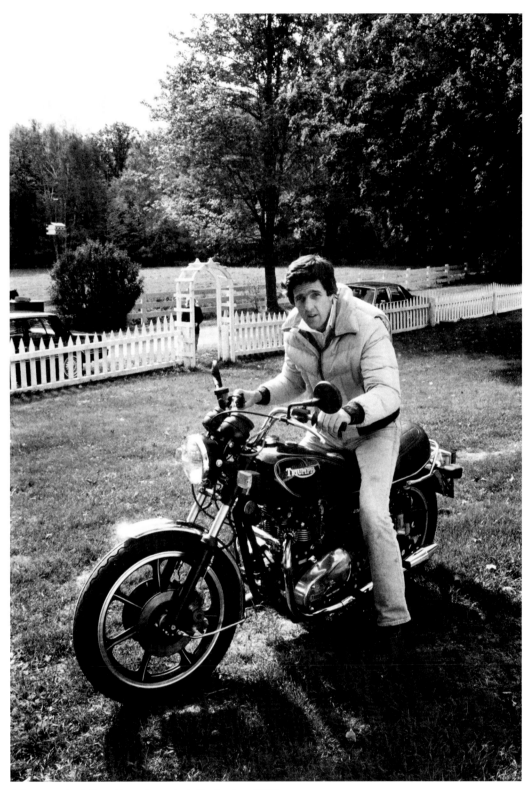

John came to visit on his motorcycle in September 1983.

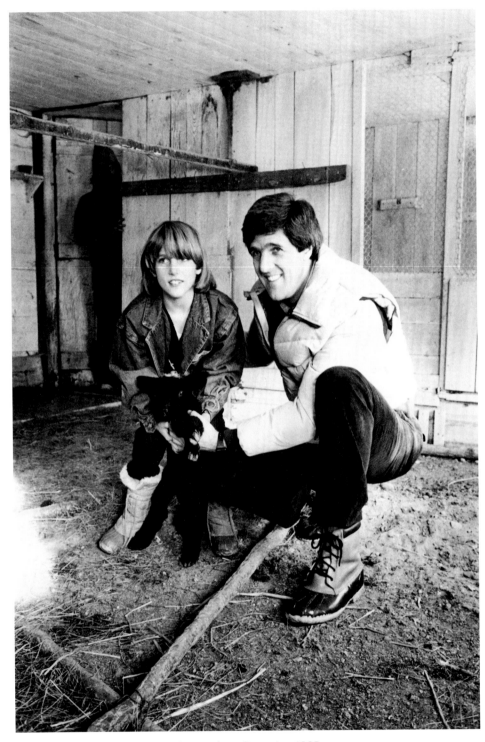

John and Vanessa with a black lamb at my farm, December 1985.

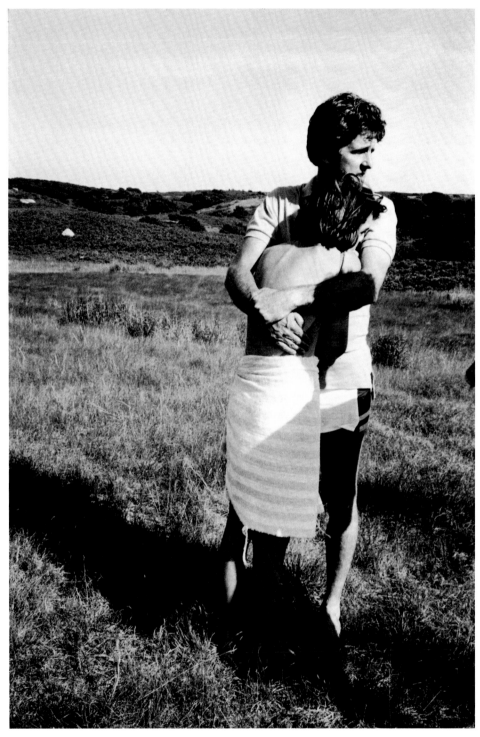

With Alex, Cape Cod, July 1987.

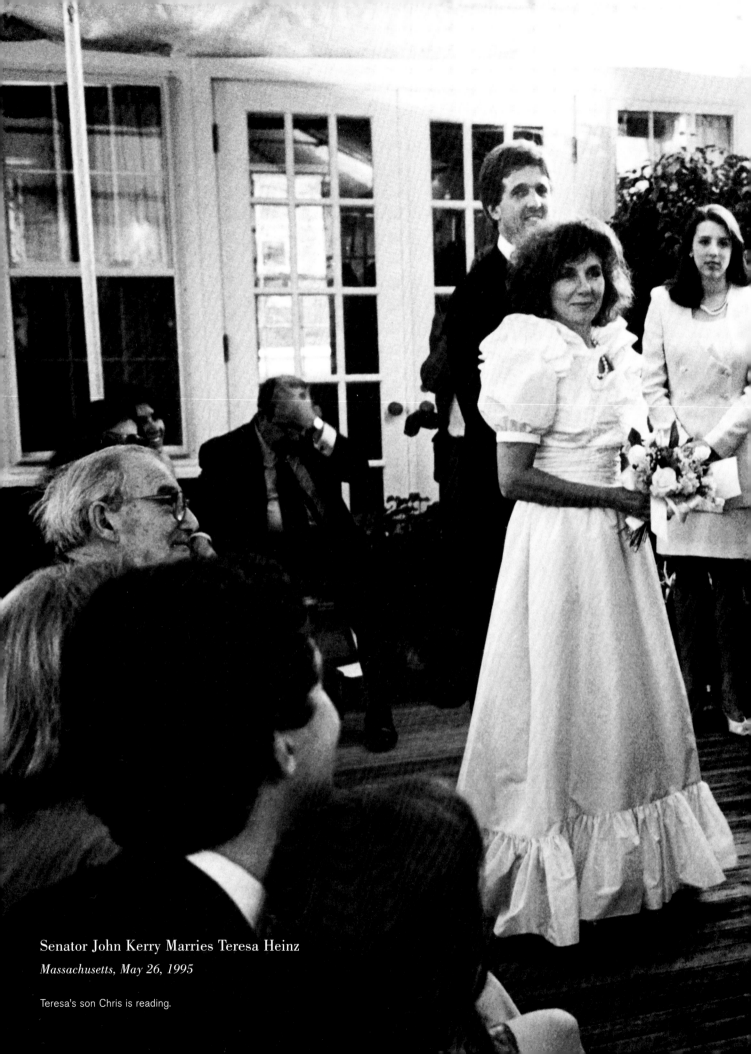

Senator John Kerry Marries Teresa Heinz

Massachusetts, May 26, 1995

Teresa's son Chris is reading.

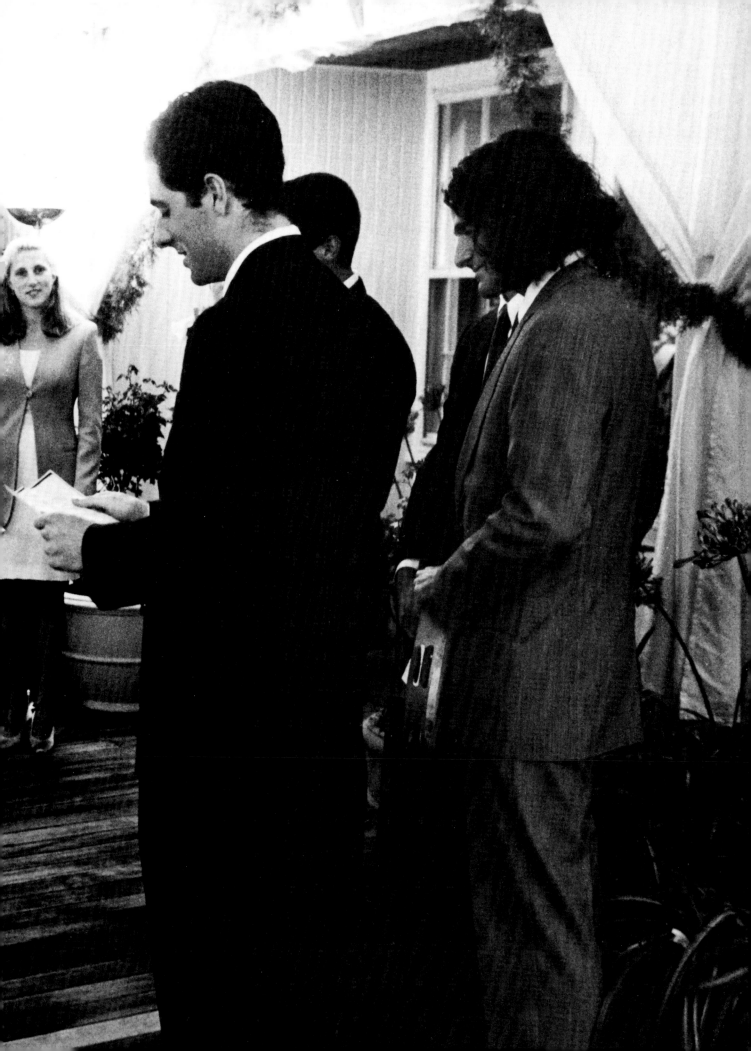

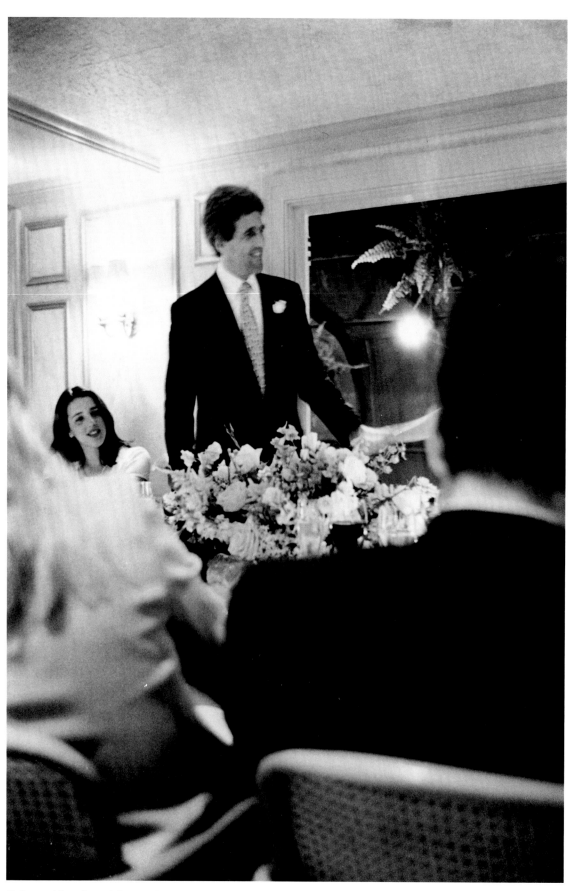

At the wedding dinner following the ceremony, John Kerry toasted his bride by reciting a poem by Shelley. Alex smiles approvingly.

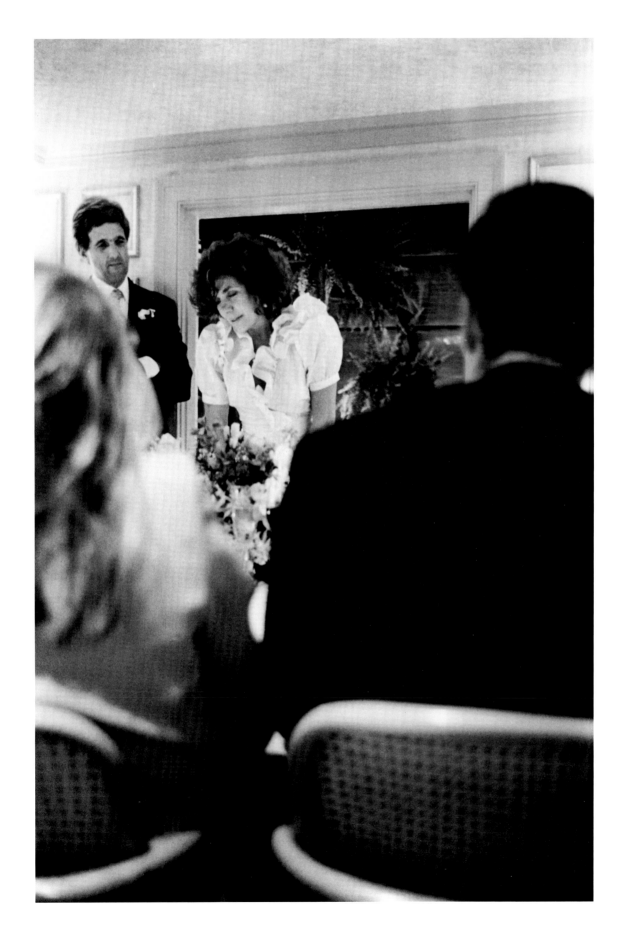

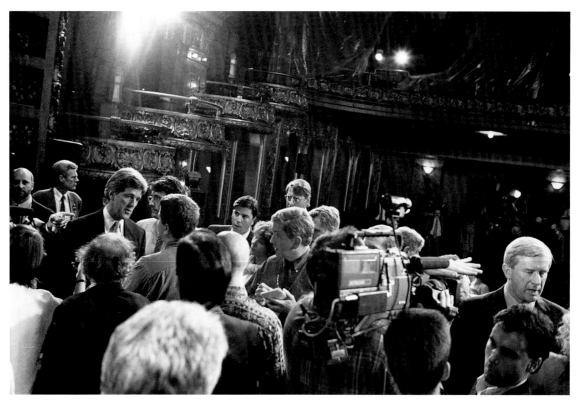

Senator John Kerry and Governor William Weld (far right), Boston Massachusetts, 1996.

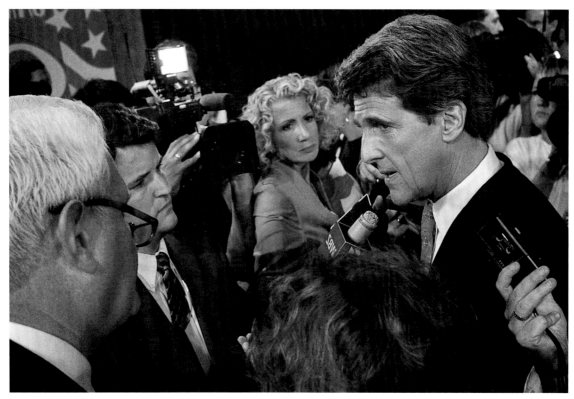

This race became the focus of national attention, pitting two bright men from old families against each other. The debates were considered remarkable for the eloquence and erudition of the two candidates. Many thought this was Kerry's tune-up race for a national campaign.

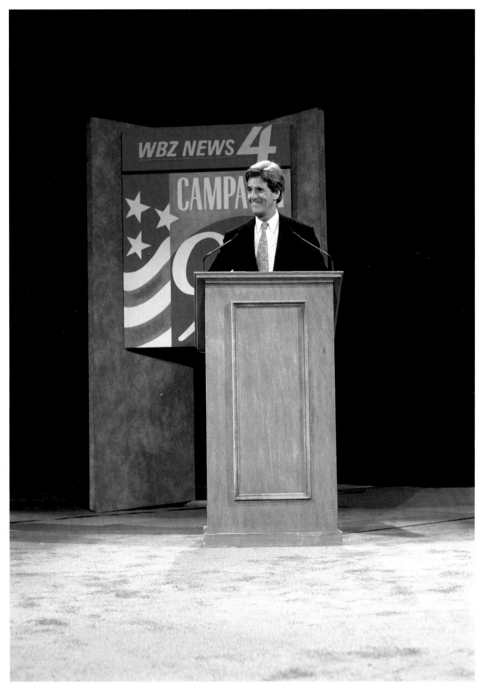

This debate took place on July 2 at the Emerson Majestic Theater in Boston. At the end of the campaign, John Kerry won reelection by a majority of 191,508 votes.

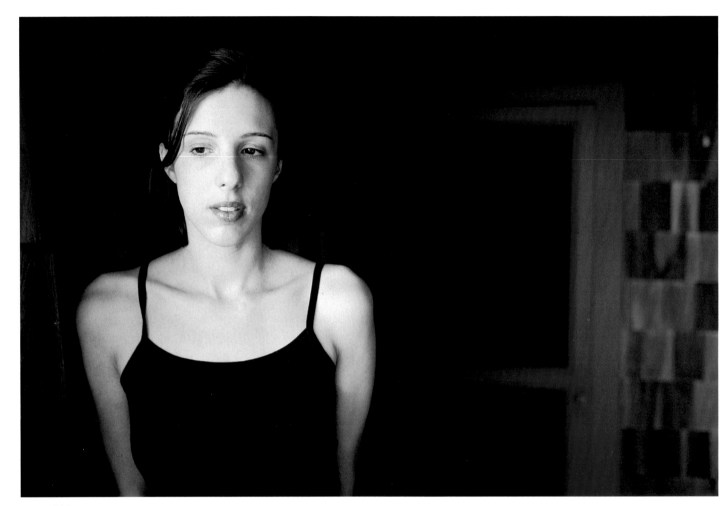

Alex, 1998.

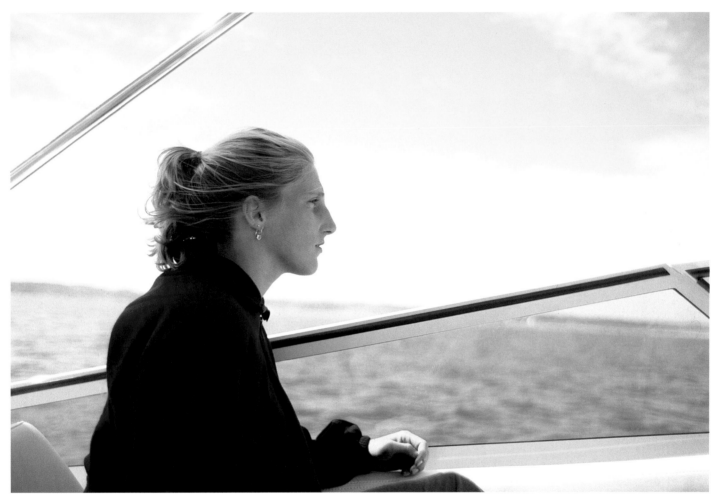

Vanessa, 1998.

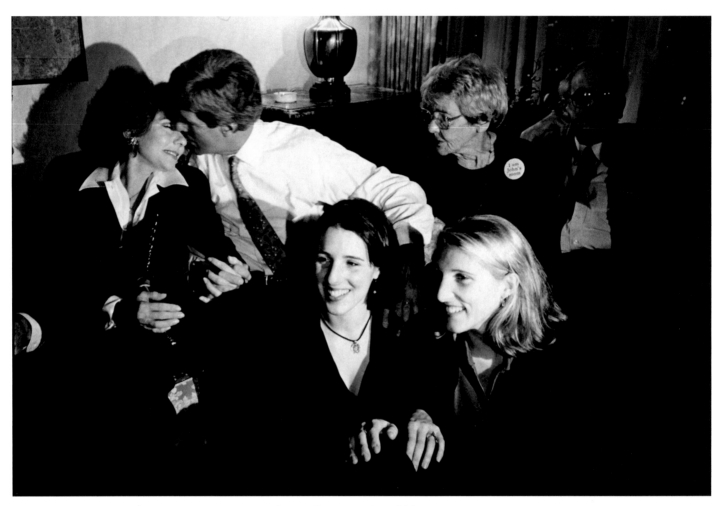

Election night. Teresa, John, Alex, Vanessa, Rosemary, and Richard Kerry, November 1996.

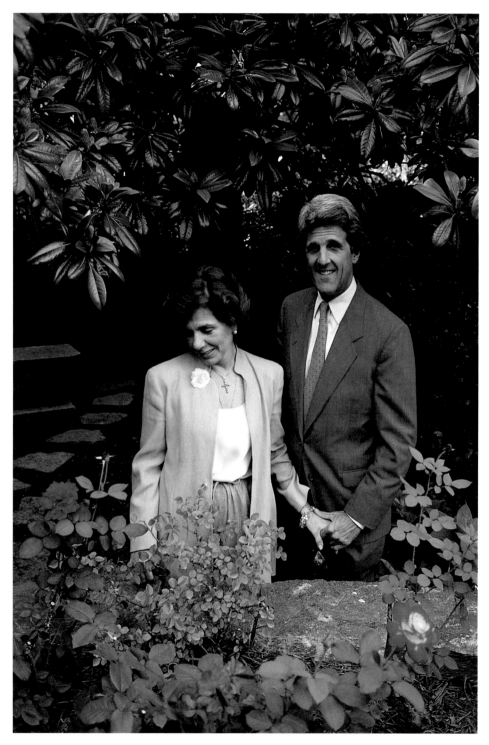

Teresa and John in their garden, Washington, D.C., 1996.

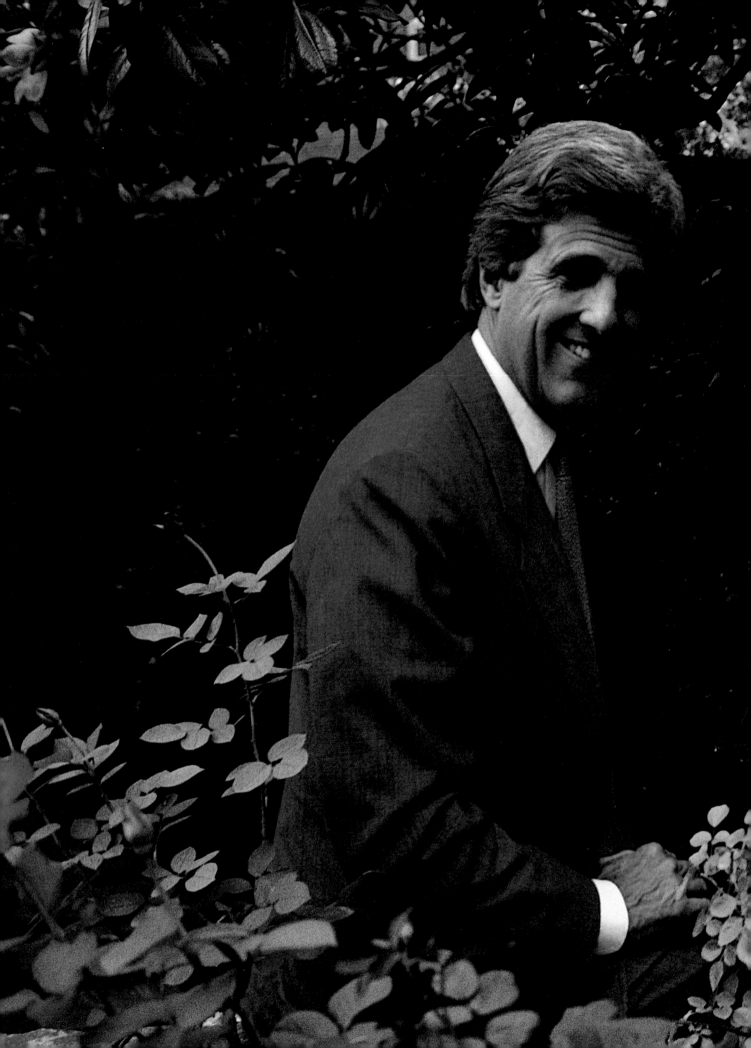

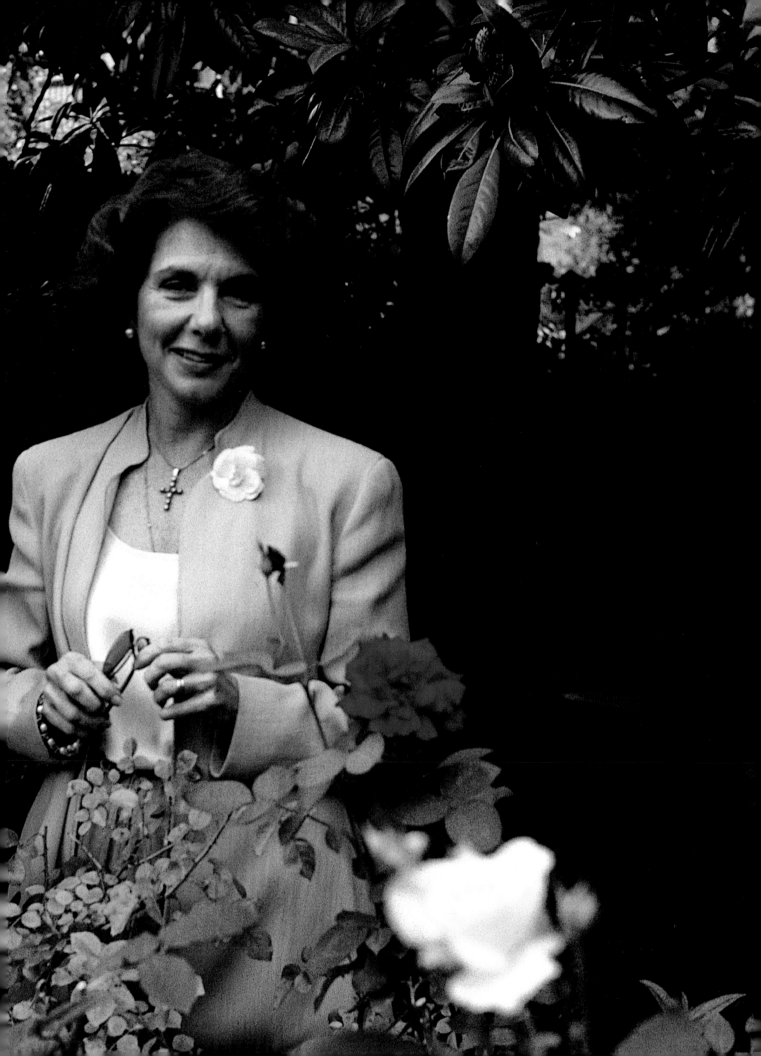

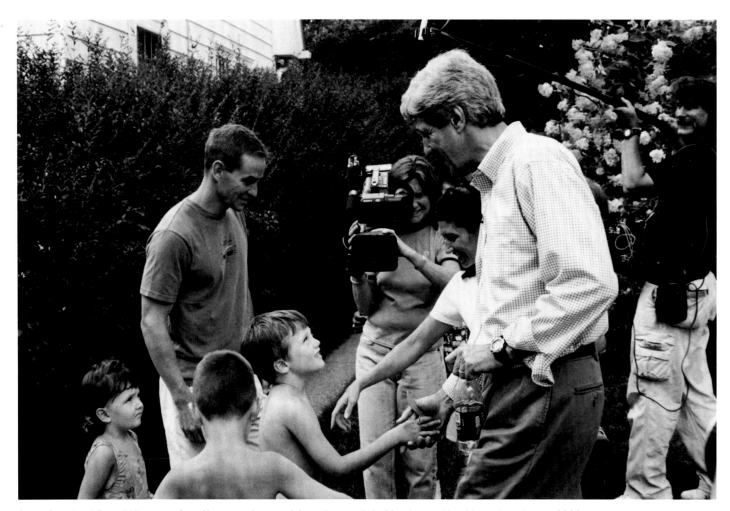

Sandi Sissel and Peter Miller, part of my film crew, shooting John with some kids. Manchester, New Hampshire, August 2003.

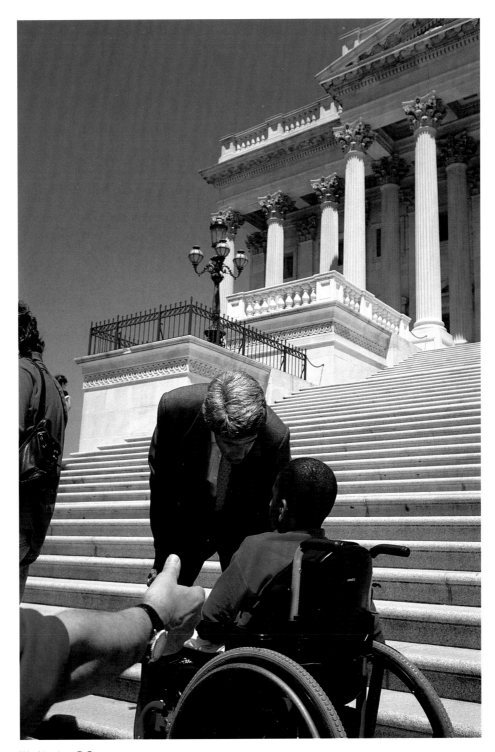

Washington, D.C.

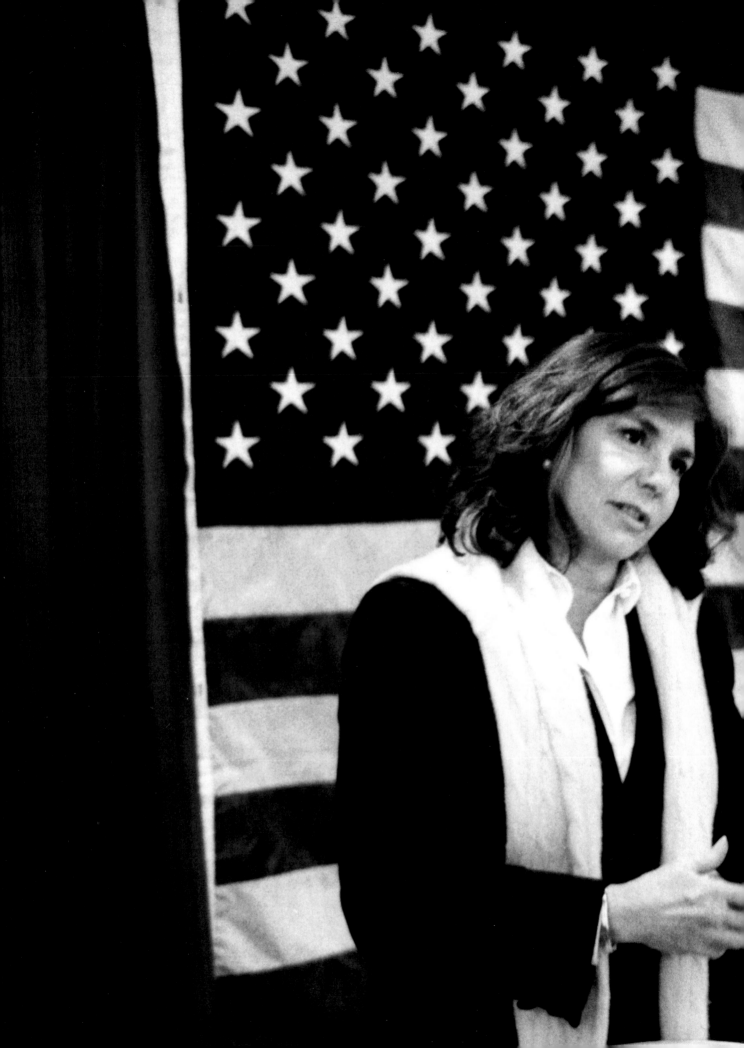

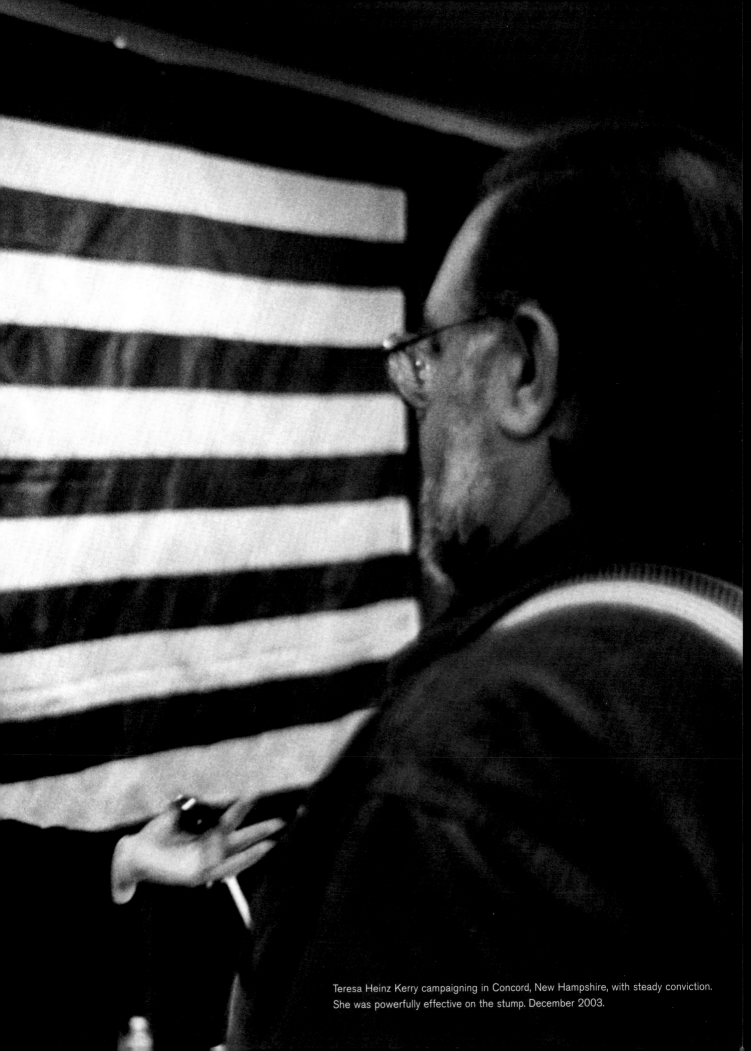

Teresa Heinz Kerry campaigning in Concord, New Hampshire, with steady conviction.
She was powerfully effective on the stump. December 2003.

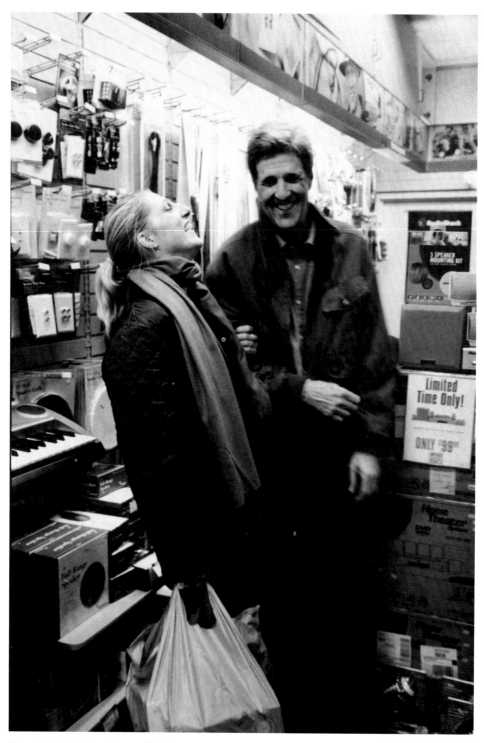

Campaigning for her father in New Hampshire, Vanessa also emerged with remarkable campaign skills,
November 2003.

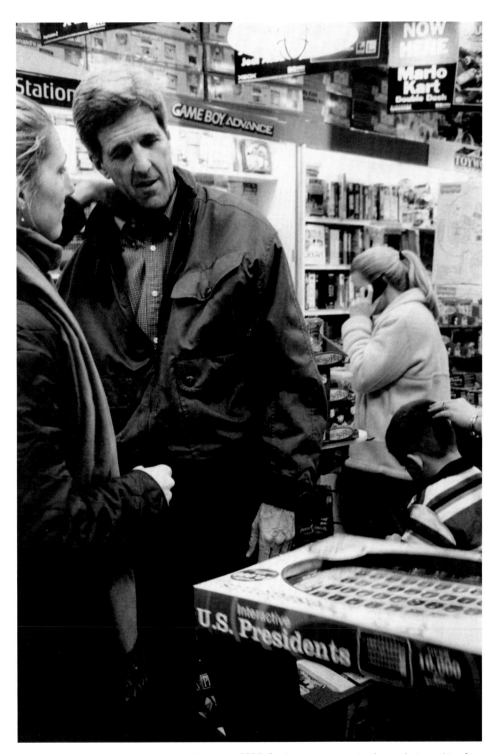

John and Vanessa Christmas shopping, November 2003. On this campaign swing I was photographing for *Time* magazine. John was at his nadir in the polls. Most people had written off his candidacy. Not Vanessa, nor I. We knew that at the moment of balance, John would always pull through.

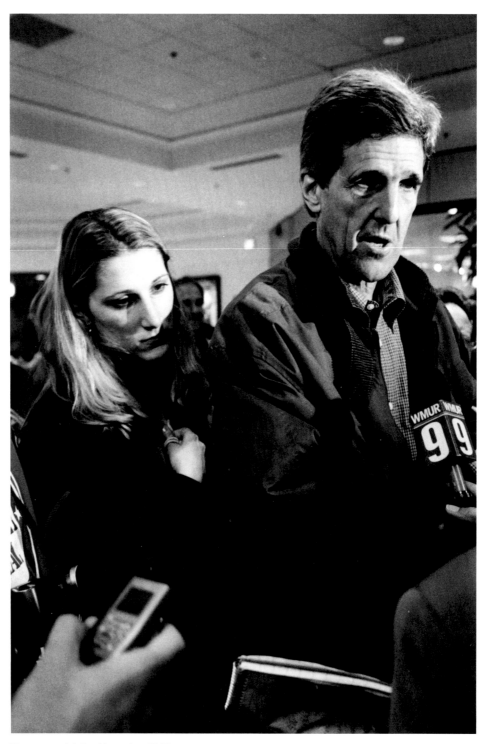

Vanessa and John, November 2003.

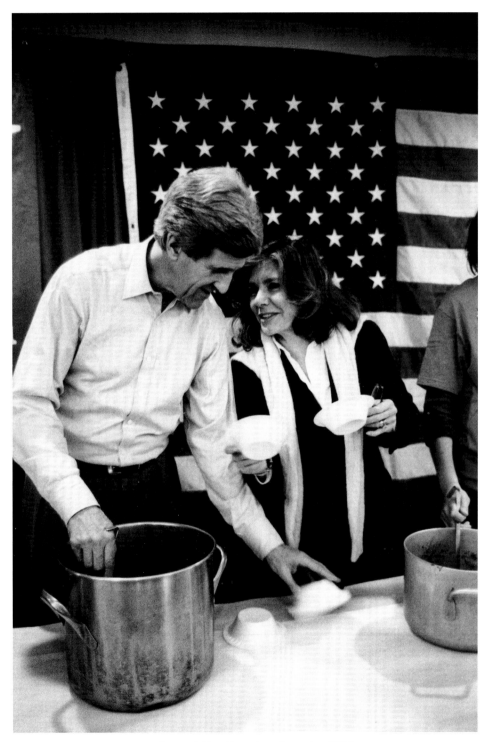

John and Teresa serving chili in Concord, New Hampshire, December 2003.

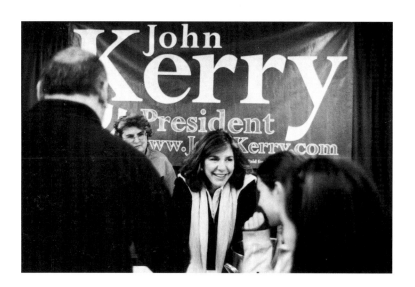

ACKNOWLEDGMENTS   I particularly wish to thank Ashley Lefrak, my photo printer and photo editor, who spent long hours going through thousands of prints and contact sheets along with my gifted designer, Kim Maley. Also my photo agent, Jeffrey Smith of Contact Press Images. No editor contributes more than Michael Sand, whose insights were essential in the conception and design of this book. Also, Peter Matson, my agent, for his quick and thorough work. And Laura Rollison, Sarah Scully, Mark Hopkins, Dan Holton-Roth, Sheridan Johns, John Dowling, and the other able associates of my company, White Mountain Films.

PHOTOGRAPHER'S NOTE   All my photographs were taken with a Leica M4 camera and a Leitz Summilex f/1.4 35 mm lens. For all black-and-white photographs I used Kodak Tri-X film. I still use the same Leica today that I began using for the first photos taken for this book in 1970. In an age in which almost all equipment is manufactured to become instantly outdated, I regard this as a significant example of thoughtful design.

Visit www.whitemoutainfilms.com for further information about the photographs.